School of Engagement

School of Engagement

45 Activities to Ignite Student Learning

Jonathan Alsheimer

ConnectEDD Publishing
Hanover, Pennsylvania

This publication is available at discount pricing when purchased in quantity for educational purposes, promotions, or fundraisers. For inquiries and details, contact the publisher at: info@connecteddpublishing.com

Published by ConnectEDD Publishing LLC
Hanover, PA
www.connecteddpublishing.com

Cover Design: Kheila Casas

School of Engagement. —1st ed. Paperback
ISBN 979-8-989-0027-8-8

ConnectEDD
PUBLISHING

Praise for *School of Engagement*

Jonathan Alsheimer's *School of Engagement* is a powerful resource for schools committed to fostering an engaging learning environment. The book's emphasis on hands-on learning for staff and students stands out, offering practical strategies that can be easily integrated into current practices. Alsheimer's approach doesn't demand a complete overhaul but instead enhances existing systems, making it feasible for any school to adopt. The book's focus on practical application ensures the concepts are theoretical and actionable. It's a fantastic tool for anyone looking to energize their school culture and improve student and staff engagement.

—Joe Sanfelippo, PhD | Educator, Speaker, and Author

School of Engagement is an exciting and motivating "reset" read for any educator. This book focuses on the important role educators play and acts as a playbook, teaching educators about how to increase and amplify their impact with actionable steps. The engaging lesson activity ideas are detailed while still being applicable for any age or grade. Both new educators and veterans can benefit from the lessons and activities laid out in this book.

—Adrienne Wiggins | Elementary Teacher

It's time to bring the magic back into the classroom! Jonathan Alsheimer has penned an essential resource for educators aiming to transform their classrooms into dynamic and interactive learning environments. His latest book offers a wealth of practical activities designed to increase student engagement, build meaningful connections, and promote collaboration. Alsheimer's innovative strategies, laid out in step-by-step format, and insightful guidance make this book a must-read for teachers seeking to inspire and motivate their students effectively.

—Eric Sheninger | Keynote Speaker and Best-Selling Author

From a teacher who walks the walk this book is a MUST READ! Mr. Alsheimer changes the way his students view learning! Walking into his classroom, I never knew exactly what to expect, but I could always count on seeing something that was fun, maybe a little crazy, and one million percent ENGAGING! That shines through in his book *School of Engagement*, a great resource for all educators.

—John Florip | Administrator

Jonathan uses his personal reflections to share practical, actionable strategies that will transform your lesson plans into dynamic learning experiences. By merging the art of engagement with the science of classroom management, School of Engagement: 45 Activities to Ignite Student Learning, provides ideas and resources to create effective, well-managed classrooms, while celebrating the joys of being an educator. Explore this book and connect with a community committed to academic excellence and innovative teaching.

—P. Sloan Joseph | Instructional Coach & Consultant

If you are looking to take classroom instruction and student engagement to the next level, Jonathan Alsheimer's School of Engagement is an absolute grand slam. With countless tips, strategies, and ideas, this book will equip you with the resources to cultivate meaningful, connected relationships in your classroom, which is the foundation for everything that we do in the world of education. *School of Engagement* is a MUST READ for anyone involved in education!

—Dr. Phil Campbell

Embrace today's K-12 student by encouraging movement, noise, and fun while also addressing grade level standards and increasing engagement with Jonathan Alsheimer's *School of Engagement: 45 Activities to*

Ignite Student Learning. As a classroom teacher, I appreciate the practicality and ease in which Alsheimer provides numerous strategies to enhance critical thinking, develop teamwork, and foster a community of creativity. New teachers will love these activities to add to their growing toolbox. Experienced educators, like me will appreciate the opportunity to grow and add fresh learning opportunities to their already successful classrooms. Trust me, Alsheimer's *School of Engagement: 45 Activities to Ignite Student Learning* will be a staple in your classroom lesson planning.

—David C. James | 7th Grade Teacher-Leader; Cabarrus County Schools, North Carolina and North Carolina Association for Middle Level Education (NCMLE) Conference and Marketing Director

School of Engagement: 45 Activities to Ignite Student Learning is an invaluable resource for educators seeking to create a dynamic learning environment where students are eager to learn and engagement flourishes. Alsheimer offers fun, practical, ready-to-use lesson activities that can be implemented immediately, ensuring a seamless transition from theory to practice. He masterfully addresses current educational challenges, providing actionable solutions that are both refreshing and evidence-based. The comprehensive framework for lesson planning and school collaboration is a standout feature, empowering educators to creatively craft engaging and memorable learning experiences. The innovative strategies and emphasis on meaningful human connections make it a must-have guide for fostering the types of experiences today's modern learners need to thrive.

—Thomas C. Murray | Director of Innovation, Future Ready Schools Best Selling Author Washington, D.C.

School of Engagement is an absolute road map to high levels of class-room engagement! Jonathan Alsheimer has put together a well thought out and detailed blueprint that will ignite creativity, enthusiasm, and high levels of learning from teachers, students, and administrators. I guarantee that this book will help jump start the passions of all who read it!

—Dan Shutes | Teacher

I highly recommend Jonathan Alsheimer's book, *School of Engagement*. As a genuine leader who speaks from the heart of a teacher, Jonathan inspires educators by highlighting the profound impact they have on their students' lives. His visits to my districts have consistently received overwhelmingly positive responses from both students and teachers. This book is filled with intentional activities and strategies that can significantly enhance the connection and teaching experience between educators and their students.

—Rose Pearson | Superintendent, Carrizo Springs CISD

Jonathan Alsheimer's new book *School of Engagement* is a MUST READ for all educators. School leaders can utilize Jonathan's school-wide framework for instructional development and teachers can build from his 45 activities to IGNITE ENGAGEMENT in the classroom. *School of Engagement* is for anyone looking to take their classroom and school to the next level.

—Hamish Brewer | Educator, Best Selling Author, and
Keynote Speaker

Mr. Alsheimer understands the essence of meaningful connections and powerful relationships — how they look, sound, and feel. He recognizes that the teacher-student relationship forms the bedrock of learning. Jonathan exemplifies these vital qualities in his book *School of Engagement*. Included are 45 highly engaging activities and a school-wide framework of collaboration providing a pathway to success, boosting motivation and sparking inspiration for learning. It's a truly magnificent and magical experience and a perfect resource for all educators!

—Dr. Deborah Hamilton Frazier | Principal

Jonathan Alsheimer is the real deal. He has a passion for transforming education and making it a place where teachers and students are excited to be. I've seen it firsthand and have used many of his strategies, ideas, and lessons to re-energize my classroom, my why, and my love for teaching. *School of Engagement* will truly make you (and help you) want to go next level in all areas to be engaging, build relationships, collaborate with colleagues, and make you want to be "that" teacher for your students!

—Jordan Fisher | K-5 Physical Education Teacher

If you want an engaging book by somebody in the trenches, who is working on a daily basis with educators, you've got to check out *School of Engagement*. Whether you're in a classroom or an administrator, this book will encourage you as you help students grow and succeed. Jonathan has come up with some ermazin activities to help you engage and ignite your kids. This is a must read for educators.

—Gerry Brooks | Educator, Speaker, and Author

Table of Contents

~

CHAPTER 1

The Challenge We Have and The Solution We Need

"Let's stop working harder and start working together!"

The Challenge: *The Redeem Team*

One of the less talked about, but captivating, stories in the world of sports is made prominent by a powerfully directed documentary on Netflix, recounting the journey of the "Redeem Team." This story, while shadowed by the legendary "Dream Team" of the Olympics past–headlined by superstars and legends of the game like Michael Jordan, Larry Bird, and Magic Johnson–presents a stirring saga. The 'Dream Team' epitomized triumph, making winning look easy. *The Redeem Team* on the other hand, symbolizes resilience. After a period of unexpected defeats and diminishing glory, the Redeem Team led the comeback and resurgence of United States basketball on the world stage at the Olympics.

While the documentary told this powerful feel-good comeback story, as an educator, I could not help but look beyond the obvious and find the small silver lining and the significant correlation to the world of

1

education. As a sports enthusiast with a love of baseball and basketball, I've always felt captivated by a true underdog story. *The Redeem Team*, featuring superstars like LeBron James, Dwayne Wade, and Kobe Bryant, and led by legendary coach Mike Krzyzewski, seemed destined for an easy victory. Yet, their journey was anything but straightforward. Although the team was composed of some of the world's greatest players, athletically gifted with abilities akin to real-life superheroes, the recent Olympic history of men's basketball on the world stage had these superheroes feeling more like underdogs.

When the team first met, Coach K was very matter-of-fact about the gravity of leading a team with such talent. Every player had superstar capabilities, but his job was to keep what they already did great. It was not to force them to do things his way. The conversation was that each player had tremendous athletic gifts and the team needed those abilities; however, the team also needed to function as a cohesive unit. Even as talented as these superstar athletes were, their abilities could only take them so far. They needed to work together and help one another continue to develop. Lebron James masterfully recounted one of the most important moments that changed the course of history for that team during their competitive quest for gold.

The turning point was a pivotal night when the players went out and engaged in team bonding—all except Kobe Bryant. Lebron explained it was a great time and the team needed that relationship-building opportunity. As the team traveled back to their hotel that morning, they arrived to find Kobe Bryant in the lobby, dressed in his workout gear and heading to the gym. The players took note, and one by one, day after day, more players joined Kobe in the gym during the early morning twilight hours. Working out together and learning from one another began to spill over onto the practice court.

As the story unfolded, players continued to do what they individually did well but also leaned on one another to improve in areas where they needed help. They still relied on the skills that had earned them their superstar status but realized that by working as a unit and learning from each other, they could become even better basketball players. In times of struggle and stress on the court, they could adjust and adapt to those situations using what they had learned from their teammates, ultimately leading them to win Olympic Gold.

While watching this story play out, I could not help but see the undertones of what teachers and educators face. We all have great abilities in relation to teaching our content and working with our students. We are professionals in our craft, well-educated and well-trained to lead a classroom with the goal of student academic achievement and educational success. That said, we are now in a situation much different from anything the world of education has ever seen, with job stresses like never before. This holds especially true when it comes to engaging students with highly effective classroom instruction day in and day out, Perhaps years ago, we felt like we were in the "Dream Team" phase of education, during which we won gold year in and year out; however, the current phase of education has fallen into a bit of a rut. What if we could change that?

Titles don't make leaders; actions do, and the time for action is now. Just like the moment when the team saw Kobe going to the gym, we need to revisit the idea of what motivates us. As the team began to work together, learning from one another, and functioning as more of a unit, they experienced tremendous success. As educators, we need to rally around each other. We must continue to use what we know is successful while having the ability to lean on the shoulders of our peers in times of struggle.

This book will serve as a roadmap to help identify areas of focus, to look outside the box in unit plan development, and provide a guide for teachers to share instructional activities. It offers an authentic and relevant look specifically related to lesson planning and in-house professional development. With various activities built into some chapters, the bulk of this book is a mixture of simple to in-depth learning activities that are not content or grade-level specific. These lessons are designed for teachers to modify and differentiate to meet the needs of their specific grade level and content, providing ideas that can be used immediately. This approach aims to relieve the pressure on teachers to develop highly engaging lessons and assist administrators in finding effective ways to support their staff and students. By leaning on each other, sharing what works, and adapting as needed, we can better meet the needs of our students. Let's stop working harder and start working together.

Why the Challenge Exists: The New Pandemic in Education

Education is in a state unlike any we've ever faced. What if we could change that? What if we could find a solution to one of the biggest problems facing educators today? There is no one-size-fits-all solution to the challenges faced by educators and schools everywhere, but what if I told you there was an answer so simple, yet untapped, by our education system that could make a real, tangible difference right now? A solution that could begin to change the narrative and direction of education, alleviating the stress on teachers. Isn't this a solution we so desperately want to see?

The truth is that teaching is unlike any other profession for many reasons, one of which is that there is never an off day. You can't walk in and say, "I'm exhausted today, so I'm going to quietly sit and answer emails and maybe make a few phone calls to clients from a comfortable chair hidden in a cubical or within an office." The reality is that at any moment, the bell is going to ring, and those children will come down the hall and into your classroom.

The profound impact a teacher can make through building relationships and ultimately shaping the future of kids is also met with the task of keeping those students motivated and engaged in the learning process. Student motivation and student engagement are vitally important, but difficult to master, yet they are driving forces for positive change in schools. The challenge of this aspect of the job is also one of the driving forces pushing not only teachers, but also administrative leaders, out of the profession.

If effectively running schools and classrooms were easy, everyone would do it. The reality is that the world of education is facing significant challenges right now. Educators are encountering a multitude of issues; some of which are new, alongside enduring challenges that have persisted over time.

Leadership teams are also contending with the impact of a "new pandemic." They face a constantly shifting landscape of instructional programs, which seem to change by the minute. Leaders are seeking practical solutions to alleviate the burden on teachers and provide immediate support for instruction.

Here is What We Can Do About It: Solution Seekers

Now is the moment for transformative action. We must revisit our motivations, much like *The Redeem Team* reimagined their approach to success. This era calls for educators to support each other, leveraging our collective strengths to overcome the challenges in education.

This book serves as a resource, guiding educators through innovative lesson planning and professional development strategies aimed at enhancing student engagement and helping teachers build meaningful relationships in the classroom. The goal is to positively impact classroom and school culture, alleviating the burden on teachers and administrators alike, by fostering an environment of shared knowledge and growth. This is true professional development that starts right down the hall.

Throughout this book, we will explore the challenges of engaging students, outline a process for schools to create a dynamic document of shared instructional strategies, and ultimately provide forty-five highly engaging and easy-to-implement activities to help get teachers started. The activities provided are to be taken and modified to fit the needs of each teacher's classroom needs. The aim is to offer a starting point for all schools to develop their practical resources to support staff and students. Take what is provided throughout this book and leverage it to enhance student engagement in your classrooms and across your school.

The call to understand the challenges in education has resonated far and wide—a familiar refrain heard in staff rooms and conferences across the globe. Yet, the era of merely identifying issues has passed; we are in the age of action and innovation. I vividly recall sitting at the desk in my classroom, embarking on unit plan development. Although I knew the content I needed to teach, I struggled with how best to teach it. At that moment, I longed to open my desk drawer or access a saved folder on my computer filled with comprehensive lesson ideas and activities. In that desperation, a vision emerged—and the solution became clear.

Imagine being a first-year or veteran teacher who inevitably reaches a point during the school year feeling drained of ideas and needing instructional inspiration. You anxiously open your top desk drawer or access a shared drive on your school computer, and there lies a heavy stack of instructional activities ready to be utilized. Whether it's a hard-copy book or a digital repository, now you have a wealth of lesson ideas to modify and use, alleviating the pressure of instructional planning.

Think of it like an encyclopedia for teachers—a comprehensive document loaded with activities, lesson ideas, games, and, most importantly, inspiration. Sometimes, drawing inspiration from someone else's developed ideas is all a teacher needs to ignite their creativity and develop something even more impactful. I remember observing a P.E. classroom where balloons were used to engage pairs and small groups of students in running and sprinting activities. Just from watching those few minutes, I gained a spark of creativity, adapting the use of balloons in my history classroom, transforming a basic worksheet review activity into a fun and interactive learning experience for students. Sharing innovative ideas like this, even if we don't always use them directly, can often spark a stroke of genius in our lesson plan development.

Generating activities specific to a particular grade level or content area can unnecessarily complicate matters and lead teachers to disregard such resources. Instead, developing a Math 7 lesson that is versatile enough to be modified for various grade levels ensures it can meet the diverse needs of all learners. Crafting lessons that transcend specific grades or subject areas empowers educators to integrate and expand upon these resources.

Rather than providing material for passive instruction, these ideas serve as a dynamic foundation. They encourage teachers to customize content, adjust difficulty levels, and vary teaching methods to align with their students' unique capabilities. This approach fosters flexibility and creativity in lesson planning, promoting effective learning experiences tailored to the unique needs of students.

To avoid the frustration of filtering through narrowly-focused or grade-specific plans, the aim is to provide straightforward and adaptable lessons that are easy to generate and open to modification and creativity. Let's keep it simple, accessible, and flexible, fostering an environment in which teachers feel supported and encouraged, and where students are actively engaged. There's no need to reinvent the wheel of student engagement but rather to share the greatness that already exists in the halls and classrooms of our schools.

This book stands as the cornerstone of that mission, offering a blueprint for an instructional renaissance—a resource guide of ideas born from the collective wisdom and creativity of educators themselves. It serves as a shared masterclass in professional development, providing a framework, outline, and solution for teachers and school leaders alike. Imagine a collaborative space where every teacher contributes and has access to a world of engaging teaching strategies—a continuous source of inspiration. This guide is shaped and reshaped by those who know the classroom best. It's more than just a resource; it's a movement toward shared academic growth.

Just as *The Redeem Team* collaborated for success, every educator within your school family will have an opportunity to participate and contribute to igniting curiosity and fostering learning through academic innovation. Similar to how Coach K leveraged the strengths of his players to achieve success on the court, we will amplify the greatness within our schools by garnishing the genius that exists in our classrooms. By building upon each other's ideas, we will expand our teacher toolbox and enrich the learning experience for our students.

This educator playbook is more than a guide; it's a call to action for teachers and leaders to unite in cultivating a dynamic document of professional growth. It's a resource that not only meets the needs of today but evolves to meet the aspirations of tomorrow.

Together, let's embark on this transformational journey, where the sharing of lesson ideas and activities becomes the heartbeat of innovation, where every lesson opens a doorway to discovery, and where every educator champions their students' success. Let's move beyond discussing the challenges in education and start implementing real solutions. With this book as a starting point, collaboration will be our strength, and student engagement will be our triumph.

Let's Discuss

In what ways could your staff meet and collaborate to share lesson and unit ideas and begin building a document of shared strategies?

CHAPTER 2

~

Meaningful Connections

"Give them a reason to show up."

The Challenge

In education, the concept of classroom community or building "relationships" often feels like a buzzword. Many teachers struggle with knowing how to build meaningful connections with their students. The challenge is real—it's not always easy to connect with students while managing all the other demands of teaching.

Building strong relationships in the classroom is crucial. While it is one of the most important cornerstones of education, it can be easier said than done. It requires effort and strategies that genuinely engage students in unique yet purposeful ways. This chapter will focus on practical methods to build these important relationships through engaging activities and effective teaching practices. These approaches can help create a positive and dynamic learning environment where students feel connected and supported, laying the groundwork for an effective learning environment for all.

Why Does the Challenge Exist?

The challenge of building authentic and meaningful relationships exists for several reasons. First, teachers often face large class sizes, making it difficult to provide individual attention to each student. In a packed schedule filled with lessons, grading, and administrative tasks, finding the time to connect on a personal level can seem nearly impossible. Second, every student is unique, bringing different backgrounds, needs, and personalities into the classroom. What works to build a relationship with one student might not work with another.

Teachers must be adaptable and sensitive to these differences, which requires additional effort and insight. Additionally, the pressures of standardized testing and curriculum demands can push relationship-building to the background. Teachers may feel compelled to prioritize academic achievement over personal connections, even though both are crucial for student success. Finally, some teachers might not feel equipped with the skills or strategies needed to build these relationships effectively. Professional development in this area can be lacking, leaving teachers to figure it out on their own.

Despite these challenges, building strong relationships is essential for a positive and effective learning environment. This chapter will provide practical solutions and strategies to help teachers overcome these obstacles and create meaningful connections with their students.

Here is What We Can Do About It

This chapter aims to provide practical solutions, offering concrete strategies and activities designed specifically to foster meaningful relationships. Here, you'll find a sample of ideas, with several additional activities included in the lesson ideas section. Engaging strategies are the bridge that invites students into the learning landscape, setting the stage for enhanced engagement.

The relationships you build and the climate you cultivate may not always start with academically driven instructional activities but rather with relationship-building opportunities. By pulling students into the learning environment through these opportunities, student engagement will naturally take flight. Fostering strong, genuine relationships within the classroom transcends the traditional academic experience. It's about establishing a learning environment in which every student feels seen, valued, and heard. When we shift our focus from solely academic pursuits to activities that prioritize relationship-building, we unlock new levels of participation. Students who might typically retreat to the background find the courage to step forward. Previously disengaged students start to feel like part of the group, becoming more willing to collaborate with peers and voice their ideas and opinions in the classroom.

By designing activities centered on relationship development rather than solely focusing on academic rigor, we invite students to open up and engage in authentic ways that transcend the textbook. The classroom transforms into a community of trust where every student feels a sense of belonging. This shift doesn't diminish the importance of academic growth; rather, it enhances it. Students who feel comfortable and valued are more likely to take academic risks, collaborate effectively with peers, and approach learning with vibrant curiosity. It is the combination of relationships, trust, and academic rigor that enhances the entire learning experience for all students.

A Closer Look: Why Can't School be More Like Disney World?

What kind of energy do you bring to the classroom? The profound nature of that question and its ramifications are deeply felt within the walls of our classrooms and schools. The nature of our work is simple, yet difficult to master: cultivating positive and meaningful relationships throughout our classroom is foundational to the work we do. It's *hard* work, but it's also *heart* work, and people should always be at the center of our efforts. Our students should always be the focal point, with the goal of building a love of learning. This cannot happen with-

> It's *hard* work, but it's also *heart* work, and people should always be at the center of our efforts.

out relationships and relationships cannot have a lasting impact in our schools without effective student engagement. The two are not mutually exclusive; rather, they work together to form a powerful bond that enhances the learning experience.

Our family is a fan of Disney, from watching the movies and shows to loving the music and taking trips to the parks, enjoying all the experiences the theme parks have to offer. When you go to a Disney theme park, it is truly unlike any place on earth. It has the total package. The vibe the moment you enter the parks is just magical. But if you look past the fancy costumes and exhilarating rides, you find a culture created unlike any other. The most important piece of that culture comes at little cost. If you have ever been to a Disney theme park, you can attest that it is the workers who create that magical feeling that overtakes you. The workers themselves have one goal: to ensure that every single person that walks into Disney has the best day of their life! I know what some people are saying: "School isn't like Disney World," or, "We don't have the funding Disney has." Some people reading this might not even like Disney, but that's not the point. I'm not talking about whether you like or dislike Disney or about their funding versus school funding. Funding aside, I'm talking about the experience we generate through something that costs absolutely nothing yet is one of the building blocks of education: How we make people feel when they walk through our doors, down our halls, into our classrooms, and the relationship that creates.

It takes zero dollars to have a warm welcome and a smile on your face when you greet your students and their families as they walk into our schools. I am quite certain that the workers at Disney parks aren't millionaires. Truth be told, they probably have a lot in common with educators. They work hard each day and often go beyond the call of duty. I believe teachers deserve to make mountains of money, and perhaps the Disney workers deserve the same. Yet, for love of what they do and through their tremendous efforts, they make a profound impact on the children and families they see day in and day out, just like educators.

The energy we bring into our classrooms and schools is the catalyst for a learning experience that is both profound and impactful. Education is a journey of the heart as much as of the mind. Relationships are the bedrock upon which this journey is built, serving as the silent pulse driving the love for learning. Without fostering strong connections, engagement cannot flourish, and without engagement, relationships weaken over time.

It's Hard Work, but It's Heart Work

I remember driving to a conference in Charlotte, North Carolina, with my family, where I was the keynote speaker. My wife and I, both teachers, had just finished a day of teaching, while my daughters came straight from school, and we were exhausted. As we arrived at the hotel late at night, we looked every bit of a mess, but the people we met made us feel like stars. They complimented my daughters, sparking such joy in them that they were excited to join the conference fun, even in their pajamas.

Reflecting on this as I prepared to speak, I thought about how these simple interactions had such a profound effect on us. They didn't cost a thing, but they made us feel valued and included. This is the energy we can bring to our schools.

As a teacher and a father, I see how important it is to build relationships. My daughters love their school because their teachers show that same joy and engagement we felt at the conference. It reminded me of Disney and how it's the people that drive the culture of any experience, and through that engagement, the atmosphere can thrive. The way we interact can invite or push away. Imagine how our actions and the relationships that develop can ultimately transform our school climate. It's about creating an environment where everyone feels valued and eager to participate. You see, relationships and student engagement go hand in hand. Together, they create an environment where students are enthusiastic and look forward to their school day and learning. This doesn't just make a difference in our classrooms; it changes how students talk about school and how they feel about Learning.

So, let's ask ourselves, what if school was more like Disney World? Not in terms of funding or flashiness, but in how we make our students feel: valued, engaged, and happy to be there. When we bring this mindset to our schools, we are more likely to see relationships blossom, engagement soar, and everyone, including teachers will be excited to be there!

The Power of Relationships

The common understanding that relationships are the foundation of the work is not a new and awe-inspiring revelation. However, one thing that slips between the cracks is the correlation between student-teacher relationships and student engagement in the classroom, and how that correlation impacts student motivation and student achievement.

Some students naturally want to build relationships with their teachers, and with some teachers, it becomes natural to do so. One of my favorite former students was a middle school student, for whom I once wrote a letter of recommendation for college. This same young man had my wife as a teacher in third grade. His memories of my wife as one of his all-time favorite teachers were inspiring, but even more compelling was his stance on learning fractions. He told me one afternoon, "I didn't work hard at fractions because I loved fractions. I worked hard at fractions because I loved Mrs. Alsheimer." He went on to tell me that because she made learning fun, the kids liked her class. That meaningful relationship formed a powerful connection that transpired into a student working hard for the love of their teacher.

Feedback from students is invaluable. It reveals the depth of their experience and shapes our approach to teaching. Our enthusiasm for the subject matter can ignite a similar zest for learning within our students. Although this can be achieved through the instructional process of teaching our content, a non-academic approach using relationship-building activities can create a similar and equally effective outcome. The result? Students eager to learn and asking, "What are we going to do tomorrow?"

This energy and passion within our schools influences the culture of our classrooms, affecting student motivation and academic achievement. It's the subtle, yet impactful, ripple effect of relationships and engagement that can either elevate or hamper the educational experience.

Build a Bridge or Drive a Wedge

The connections forged between students and teachers through an engaging classroom can build a bridge to a love of learning or drive a wedge that stifles curiosity and motivation. Captivating activities play a pivotal role in this dynamic, because they can inspire or dispirit students, influencing their perception of school and their eagerness to learn. Creating a welcoming atmosphere from the first day is crucial, akin to the magical first steps and experiences at Disney. However, it's the engaging instruction that sustains and deepens these relationships. Whether it's a student who blossoms through participation or the reluctant child who finds a voice, the instructional approach can make all the difference. Striking the balance between fostering relationships and maintaining classroom management is key. Engaging relationship-building activities can be effective and enjoyable ways to build connections while preserving the educational structure.

Establishing class norms, routines, and setting clear expectations and boundaries is a complex task for educators. It's a balancing act, harmonizing the chorus of "relationships, relationships, relationships" that echoes the educational philosophies of many educators, while simultaneously addressing the demands of classroom management. I, too, share the sentiment that relationships are a crucial pillar of educational success, because they form the foundation from which student growth emerges.

Nevertheless, I also uphold the principle that effective classroom management is the framework within which these relationships can flourish. It sets the stage and lays the groundwork for a structured yet dynamic learning environment. Without it, not only is relationship-building compromised, but also the ability to keep students actively engaged in learning is lessened.

The challenge, then, is to create a classroom culture in which relationships are nurtured without disrupting the essential structures and routines that support learning. One of the most effective approaches is to introduce activities that captivate students' interests and allow for authentic interactions. For example, utilizing resources as simple as red plastic solo cups, note cards, yarn, and rubber bands can generate a host of activities that can be game-changers. These versatile tools offer a low-cost solution to relationship-building and lesson planning that can be adapted in various ways. They provide a platform for students to connect with the material, with their teacher, and with one another, reinforcing the collaborative spirit and classroom routines essential to a thriving educational environment.

Relationship Building Sample Activities

Here are a few sample relationship-building activities that can be used directly or to inspire new ideas. This is a small sample, but these strategies are among my favorites for building relationships and can be implemented at the beginning of the year or anytime you want to enhance community in your classroom.

SAMPLE LESSON Activity 1: "Tower of Terror"

My day one, week one, or random Friday to build relationships, have fun, and create an inclusive classroom culture activity is called "Tower of Terror," named after the Disney theme park ride because of their similarity. If played correctly, it brings out an energy and the kind of positive environment that pulls students in. This activity also gets students smiling, laughing, and fully engaged, often asking, "Can we do this again tomorrow?" The best part is you can modify this kind of activity for any age and grade level.

Objective:
Students will participate in the following relationship building activity called "Tower of Terror" which encourages teamwork, strategy, and fine motor skills. This activity is designed to energize the class and foster a positive competitive spirit.

Materials:
  + Plastic cups (enough to create stacks 3-4 cups high for each group)
  + Sturdy large notecards (one for each gap in the cup stacks)

Activity Overview:

The "Tower of Terror" is an engaging activity that can be adapted for any age group. It simulates the excitement and suspense of the Disney theme park ride with the same name and a similar outcome. The goal is to carefully pull notecards from between stacked cups without causing the tower to fall. Each successful attempt getting all cups in the stack to drop together results in a point for the group. I add points of all groups in each class together during each round to generate a total. Round times are three minutes each. With classes working together to beat the total score of my other classes now we are creating a "team" or "family" component to the activity. Each class works together to beat other classes' scores rather than competing against each other and causing division.

Setup Instructions:
1. Stack the plastic cups 3-4 high, inserting a notecard between each cup.
2. Ensure notecards are strong and not cut pieces of paper for stability.

Rules of the Game:
1. Players will take turns pulling out one notecard each or they can pull on the "Count of 3" but each player pulls a different card.
2. If pulling a notecard causes the cups to fall sideways, the player responsible is "out" if it is a 1 on 1 game. If it is a group game, they just restack the cups as quickly as possible and continue playing until the timed round ends.
3. If the cups drop but remain stacked the team or individual earns 1 point.
4. The objective is to remove all notecards so that the cups collapse straight down together.

Game Variations:
+ Student vs. Student
+ Student vs. Teacher
+ Group vs. Group
+ Whole Class vs. Teacher
+ Whole Class vs. Whole Class (e.g., Period 1 vs. Period 3)
+ Tournament Play: Form groups of 4-6; one student from each group advances after each round.
+ Hold a championship round with the final two students.

Skill-Building and Time-Limited Challenge:
+ Allow students time to practice becoming familiar with the game and how to successfully get the cups to drop.
+ Introduce a time-limited challenge where groups must reach a set goal within 3-5 Minutes.

Scoring and Competition:
+ Keep a cumulative score for the class as they work in groups. Ask groups to call for your attention so you see the cups successfully dropped each time to raise the energy level in the class and to keep an accurate continuous score.
+ Announce the time and maintain the pace as students attempt to beat the best score of the day.
+ Create a class leaderboard to foster healthy competition between classes. This is a great way to keep kids energized during the activity. Playing upbeat music also helps.

Closure:
Conclude the activity with a discussion on strategies used, reflections on teamwork, and observations about the energy and positive collaboration among students. Use this as a moment to mention how learning and class can be fun, but that it depends on how students react to each

other and to the learning environment. Be sure to explain that learning can be engaging and fun or boring and students' reactions, responses to each other, and actions during these games will determine the activities you decide to use throughout the year.

Assessment:
Evaluate students on participation, teamwork, and the ability to strategize effectively during the game.

SAMPLE LESSON Activity 2:
The Almost Impossible Cup Pyramid

Objective:
Students will engage in a team-building exercise that challenges their collaboration, cooperation, and problem-solving skills. The activity requires groups to construct various pyramid structures using red solo plastic cups, with the ultimate challenge of building the almost impossible pyramid.

Materials:
- Six red plastic solo cups per group
- One rubber band large enough to fit around the cups per group.
- One piece of yarn (8-12 inches long) per student. I like to use yarn rather than string because yarn is easier to hold and less likely to rip the rubber band during the activity.

Activity Overview:
The "Impossible Cup Pyramid" is a collaborative relationship and team building activity that tests students' ability to work together to manipulate objects using indirect methods. The task is to construct a series of pyramid structures made up of red plastic solo cups as first

demonstrated by the teacher, culminating in an advanced structure of cups deemed "the almost impossible pyramid."

Setup Instructions:
1. Form groups of four or five students.
2. Distribute six cups, one rubber band, and one piece of yarn per student to each group.

Rules of the Game:
1. Each student ties their piece of yarn to the rubber band, spacing the yarn evenly around it.
2. Each student must have only one piece of yarn but can trade at any time to aid in moving the cups or successfully building the pyramid.
3. Students can only hold their piece of yarn and are not allowed to touch the cups directly with their hands or any part of their body.
4. Movement, trading yarn, and strategizing are allowed, as long as students do not touch the cups with their bodies.
5. If the cups fall, students can only then pick them up to restack and start over. To allow for greater success and activity buy-in, I allow a dropped or fallen cup to be returned to the stack but not restack all the cups.
6. The initial goal is to deconstruct a stack of cups and arrange them into a pyramid shape.

Pyramid Challenges:
- Start with a basic pyramid structure of three cups at the base, two in the middle, and one on top.
- Progress to a layer of three upright cups, with three inverted cups balanced on top.

+ Introduce more complex pyramids, leading up to "the almost impossible pyramid" where all six cups are stacked vertically, one on top of the other.

Closure:
Discuss the challenges faced, the importance of communication, and the strategies that led to successful pyramid construction.

Assessment:
Evaluate the groups on their ability to work cohesively, their strategy development, positive collaboration, and their success in constructing the pyramid structures as the rounds progressed and the pyramids became progressively more difficult.

SAMPLE LESSON Activity 3: The Scribe

Objective:
Students will engage in a collaborative activity designed to foster communication, cooperation, and fine motor skills. "The Scribe" requires students to work together to write or draw with a marker controlled by yarn attached to a dry erase marker using painters' tape.

Materials:
+ One piece of painters' tape about 6-8 inches long (I like painters' tape because it's easier to use and sturdier)
+ One piece of yarn (8-12 inches long) per student
+ One dry erase marker per group
+ Something to write and draw on (large paper, desk, or whiteboard)

Activity Overview:
In "The Scribe" students are tasked with writing or drawing on a desk, large paper, or whiteboard using a dry erase marker that is manipulated

indirectly through yarn attached by tape. The activity emphasizes teamwork and the development of interpersonal relationships and both verbal and non-verbal collaboration.

Setup Instructions:
1. Organize students into groups.
2. Provide each group with tape, a piece of yarn for each student, and a dry erase marker.
3. Have students tie or connect their yarn to the dry erase marker in any way they wish, distributing the yarn with enough slack to be used but not physically touching the marker.

Rules of the Game:
1. The dry erase marker is placed standing upright on the desk.
2. Students must only hold their piece of yarn and cannot touch the marker directly with their hands or any part of their body once it has been taped and the activity has begun.
3. The group must work together to move the marker and write or draw the assigned task.
4. If the marker falls, students can reset it upright.
5. The goal is for the group to use the marker to write a number, word, or draw a simple picture as assigned by the teacher.
6. To advance the difficulty level during a given round, do not allow verbal communication. Finally, for the most difficult round, allow verbal communication but eyes must be closed, and students must talk it out. **Task Examples:**
   + Write a specific number or series of numbers.
   + Write a word or a short sentence.
   + Draw a simple picture, such as a snowman.

Closure:
Conclude with a group discussion about the strategies that were effective, the challenges of working together, and the importance of communication in collaborative tasks.

Assessment:
Evaluate student groups based on their ability to collaborate, communicate, and successfully complete the writing or drawing task.

Tidal Wave of Change

Just as Disney captures the hearts and minds of all who step through its gates—not just through roller coasters but through the magic and love of its workers—we, too, have the power to create magic within our schools by viewing education through a new lens that emphasizes the transformative power of relationships. Not as a mere buzz word but as a call to action. This perspective demands a shift from conventional teaching to a realm where every corner of the classroom bursts with energy and engagement, much like the alluring streets of Disney World.

Imagine the first day of school, not as a mundane routine, but as an exciting event where students are ushered into an adventure, walking away after day one asking the question, "Can we do that again tomorrow?" This is the moment where the tone is set, where the ordinary learning environment transforms, and where every subsequent day becomes an opportunity to reinforce that learning can be engaging and fun.

Moving through the year, let's break the status quo and look at the bigger picture of education. Beyond our content areas, let's view our classrooms as opportunities to make a daily impact. Let's craft strategies that embrace outside-the-box thinking to capture the hearts and minds of our students. Educators can collaborate, developing and sharing relationship-building activities, each designed to draw students into a world of curiosity and an eagerness to learn. These activities are more than icebreakers; they are purposeful tools to captivate and impart larger lessons. They reinforce that our classrooms are communities of collaboration and shared ideas, where we learn not only academic content but also valuable character lessons from each experience.

> These activities are more than icebreakers; they are purposeful tools to captivate and impart larger lessons.

The effects are profound, with ripples that serve a purpose in multiple facets of our classrooms throughout the school year. Students are no longer mere attendees but active participants, energized and ready for the day's lessons. This enthusiasm for content seamlessly translates into a passion for the classroom itself. The student-teacher bond strengthens, and with each engaging lesson, a deeper connection is formed. Student engagement and relationships are not isolated but work collectively to enhance the educational experience for everyone. Together, they elevate classroom and school culture, enhance motivation for students and teachers alike, and, most of all, ignite a passionate love for learning.

As this movement to build a love of learning gains momentum, it sweeps through the halls like a tidal wave, instilling a palpable shift not only in our classes but in the climate and culture of our building. Schools no longer feel like institutions; they become places of warmth and wonder where everyone's ideas are welcome. Teachers are smiling and students are excited about the day. We no longer hear phrases like, "living the dream" or "another day in paradise" as sarcastic undertones, but rather, we actively participate in building that paradise.

Let's Discuss

In what ways have you seen instruction play a role in the relationships between students and teachers in your school? How has it impacted your classroom/school and the learning environment and relationships between you and your students?

CHAPTER 3

~

The Ripple Effect: How Student Engagement Can Lead to Self-Managed Classrooms

"Insanity is doing the same thing over and over again expecting different results."

–Albert Einstein

Collaborative Strategies for Dynamic Classroom Management

As you read through the pages of this chapter, you will find a celebration of the collective spirit of teaching and the embrace of student engagement as the cornerstone of an effective classroom. Imagine a place where the walls resonate with the sounds of enthusiastic learning, and classrooms burst with the joy and smiles of students and teachers. This isn't just a dream—it's the reality we craft together when we merge the art of engagement with the science and precision of classroom management to create an atmosphere overflowing with a curiosity for learning and mutual respect.

As we continue to examine our educational practices, focusing on how to effectively and collaboratively collect and share strategies to enhance student engagement, it is important to acknowledge a gap often left unfilled by our formal training: classroom management. Reflecting on my own academic career, I realized that despite completing an undergraduate degree and two Master's programs, I spent minimal time mastering one of the most critical aspects of teaching: how to effectively manage a classroom full of students with diverse backgrounds and varied social, emotional, and educational needs.

Throughout my years in the classroom, I have witnessed the transformative effect of engagement. A well-managed academic environment may be one of the more complex puzzles of classroom management. One of the most effective ways to build and maintain relationships and cultivate a positive classroom culture is by getting students excited about their learning.

When learning flourishes, teaching becomes even more rewarding. With each spark of interest and every moment of engagement, the transformation of teaching is evident—where learning is no longer a task but a shared adventure. By pooling our resources and experiences, we can create a living document of instructional strategies—a compilation of ideas that serves as a framework, guiding us toward more engaging, effective, and joyful teaching experiences. No one understands the unique challenges and triumphs

> No one understands the unique challenges and triumphs of a classroom better than fellow educators. For this very reason, the importance of collaboration cannot be overstated.

28

of a classroom better than fellow educators. For this very reason, the importance of collaboration cannot be overstated. Together, we possess an extensive wealth of knowledge, filled with years of strategies that, when shared, can alleviate the individual stresses and frustrations of lesson planning.

This collaborative approach is not just about sharing what works; it's about shouldering the collective responsibility of building something special in our school. It's about relieving the pressure that comes with the search for continual engagement and allowing us to breathe life into our lessons without the constant strain of finding ways to innovate in isolation. It's not just a content or grade level but a schoolwide collaboration of knowledge and pedagogical successes.

As you dive into the insights and activities within this chapter and throughout this book, remember that you are not alone. We are a community of educators, united in the pursuit of academic and behavioral excellence. Welcome to transformative innovation in teaching, where the collective crafting of authentic and relevant teaching ideas captivates and inspires both teacher and student alike. The result? The challenges relating to classroom management become easier to navigate.

Same Kids, Different Results

We can't get students excited about learning if we can't get to the part where they are learning. In the classroom, there is an obvious correlation between student engagement and behavior management. When teachers execute well-developed instructional activities, disciplinary problems begin to decrease, and, in some cases, almost disappear entirely. To ensure our students are successful and achieve academically, we must understand this correlation and adapt our teaching methods, use our resources, and continually develop the learning atmosphere. We need to be willing to use activities provided by other great teachers and be eager to try new things to find what works best with our teaching styles and our student populations. By doing so, we give ourselves the best opportunities to engage students in our lessons and alleviate the pressures and stress of constant classroom disruptions.

Think about the best class you ever had and simultaneously think about the worst. Growing up, I had several great classes and teachers, however, the ones I remember the most are the classes where the teacher made learning fun. We were so engaged in the activities that we forgot we were even learning. The sad, yet interesting, thing is that many of those same students who were fully engaged in one classroom would go to the next classroom and behave completely differently, displaying off-task behaviors, disruptive conduct, and inattentiveness. It was as though they were completely different kids altogether. In one classroom, the teacher rarely had to correct anyone, while in the other, it was disorderly chaos and disrespect.

In my early days of teaching, like many educators, keeping students focused while managing the classroom presented real challenges. I used to struggle to keep my students' attention and deal with the constant interruptions that impeded everyone's learning. It was frustrating, especially since I knew I was the one who had control over the outcome. My classroom routines were in place, but my teaching and instructional methods needed work. I was an engaging teacher, but inconsistent. Over time, I picked up new ideas from fellow educators, became more creative in my own quest to develop activities, continued enhancing my teaching strategies, and eventually, the learning conditions began to change.

The classroom and academic environment became a different place altogether. The boredom my students once experienced, which often led to disruptions, was replaced by newfound curiosity. I found myself enjoying teaching more because I was increasingly absorbed in the lessons. Behavior problems nearly disappeared because the activities students engaged in were so compelling that they would all lose track of time. What truly changed was not my students or my routines, but how I taught and the consistent use of interactive activities. Looking back, I can see just how much more effective I could have been from the start if I had these strategies and insights earlier in my teaching career.

Instructional Planning: A Deeper Look

Educators often get caught up with the words "engaging" and "fun" as though they are two separate things, but I tend to think differently. I believe they are one and the same. Think back on the most exciting times in your life. The moments when we are most engaged in an activity are often the times in life when we are having fun. In my own experience, I can recall times when I was having so much fun and was so engaged in a moment that I almost shut the world out and forgot what was going on around me because I was so focused.

The best thing we can do for our students is to make our classes and schools a place they want to be—where they feel safe being themselves and can enjoy learning. The key to achieving this is through cultivating a learning environment with minimal classroom disruptions, where students can focus and flourish. It's an environment where students are actively engaged in their learning, which simultaneously relieves pressure on the teacher and naturally assists in classroom management. These are the true benefits of highly engaging instruction. Like Albert Einstein says, "Insanity is doing the same thing over and over again expecting different results." If we want different and perhaps more successful outcomes, we need to adapt and adjust our schoolwide instructional practices, because the best classroom management strategy is a great lesson plan.

The Magic of Engagement

Think about a time when you were completely absorbed in an activity. Chances are, you weren't causing trouble, feeling restless, or

31

disconnected. That's what engagement can do for your students. When students are genuinely interested in what they are learning, behavior problems can often take care of themselves. Here's the good news: by prioritizing student engagement, not only can you create a more effective learning environment, but you can also significantly improve classroom management. Let's dive into some practical strategies:

Clear Expectations: Set the stage for engagement by clearly defining your expectations for students, both in terms of behavior and participation. I often begin class by introducing the essential question or key takeaway I want the students to remember by the end of our time together for the day. By modeling behavior, engaging in conversations about the importance of teamwork, and providing engaging activities which lead to more enjoyable learning experiences, we continuously reinforce the behaviors we want to see. This approach also empowers students by placing ownership of the activity on them, giving them a sense of responsibility for the outcomes.

Positive Reinforcement: Recognize and reward engagement. This could be as simple as offering verbal praise or implementing a point system that leads to classroom privileges. Consider rewarding the whole class for the actions of one student rather than punishing the whole class for the actions of a single student. This approach fosters whole-class buy-in, improves classroom culture, and encourages other students to emulate the rewarded behaviors.

For example, if Jacob forgot his materials but remembered the correct procedure to get paper and a pencil and started on the assignment right away, you might say, "Because Jacob showed responsibility, I'm going to reward the whole class by..." and then provide the reward. This approach can also apply to group interactions or successful completion of activities where you might promise a reward like a game, a fun story, no homework, a smaller assignment, extra recess or ten minutes of technology time at the end of class, depending on age and grade-level. These small investments can yield significant benefits in the long run.

Consistent Routines: The key here is consistency. In any situation or activity in life, knowing what is expected leads to greater engagement and success. In our classrooms, establish a rhythm and routines that students can anticipate and predict. When students know what to expect, they are more likely to engage actively in their learning.

Engagement as Intervention: If a student starts to act out, redirect their energy by actively engaging them in the lesson. Ask for their opinion or offer them a role in the activity. Students value ownership, choices, and having a voice, so involving them in an activity gives them a chance to feel invested in the lesson. This approach can help shift their focus positively and foster a more productive learning environment.

Reflection Time: Allow time for students to reflect on what they've learned and how they have participated. This can include a short conversation about the continuation of fun engaging activities, discussing ways in which student behavior contributed positively during a lesson, and how that positive behavior can lead to more similar activities in the future. Reflection serves to reinforce engagement and give students a sense of accomplishment.

Effective Icebreakers Make a Difference: The role of simple yet effective icebreaker activities in classroom management is often underestimated. Many educators overlook these activities because they may seem lacking in content, not varied enough, or only suitable for the beginning of the school year. However, purposeful icebreaker activities can be used at any time to enhance student engagement and contribute to a positive classroom environment, thereby supporting effective classroom management.

Activities like the "Tower of Terror," "The Almost Impossible Cup Pyramid," and "The Scribe," as mentioned in this book, or other creative activities such as creating rainbow designs with Skittles and dish soap, serve as opportunities for reflective discussions where students can identify and share their unique qualities. These conversations foster connections and unity within the class.

Furthermore, interactive games like the speed math challenge, where students pair up and compete in basic on-the-spot addition or multiplication, encourage lively participation. These activities can be formatted in various ways, such as tournaments or a playful teacher-versus-students challenge, adding an element of fun and engagement to the learning process.

Know Their Interests: Start by understanding the passions of your students. I often integrate student interests into lessons. For instance, during a geography unit when students needed to learn about U.S. states and regions, I leveraged their love for video games and role-playing. I introduced an activity called "Zombie Apocalypse Geography," on Wednesday, explaining how their work from Monday and Tuesday would be used. The more we align our lessons with student interests, the greater the surge in engagement, leading to positive behavior, and increased student buy-in as the norm.

Variety is the Spice of Learning: Clear and consistent expectations and routines are essential, but it is also crucial to vary your teaching methods. Incorporate games, debates, group work, challenges, creative writing, project-based learning, and technology including the use of AI, among others. Changing the pace keeps students engaged and eager to participate, and they will navigate through the less exciting parts of learning knowing that engaging activities are on the horizon.

Real-World Connections: The more authentic and relevant a lesson is to students' lives outside the classroom, the more invested students become. Show students how lessons apply practically, such as using math to build structures like engineers or creating their own businesses with advertising and marketing strategies. Encourage students to utilize AI (Artificial Intelligence) tools to develop more efficient and realistic projects that showcase their knowledge and its application in real-world scenarios. When students understand the relevance of what they are learning, they are more likely to be motivated and engaged in their studies.

Student Choice: Give students some control over their learning process. Offer them options to choose from a list of projects or allow them to decide how they want to demonstrate their understanding. Choice boards are an effective method for implementing this approach. Even if the assignment is challenging, providing students with autonomy in selecting their tasks or assessments reduces disruptions and enhances their curiosity and interest in the subject matter. This autonomy fosters a sense of ownership and responsibility, which can lead to greater engagement and motivation to excel in their learning endeavors.

Collaborative Learning: Encourage teamwork and peer grouping among students. Peer support can significantly boost confidence, motivation, and interest in learning. While assignments and assessment can be done individually, let students know they can draw on their peers' ideas and support each other. This approach not only makes instruction less challenging for the teacher but also allows students to access the assistance they need from their peers, especially if they are hesitant to appear vulnerable in front of the teacher or the whole class.

The 3 C's - Collaboration, Creativity, and Critical Thinking: Authentic and relevant activities that align with educational standards and objectives have the potential to significantly transform classroom dynamics. Integrating the "3 C's" (Collaboration, Creativity, and Critical Thinking) into instructional planning can greatly enhance student engagement and deepen their understanding of content.

This approach can be effectively implemented through project-based and inquiry-based learning methods. These methodologies emphasize authentic tasks that resonate with students' interests and real-world relevance, thereby promoting student choice and ownership over their learning journey. By fostering collaboration among students, encouraging creative problem-solving, and promoting critical thinking skills, educators can create a dynamic learning environment that supports meaningful learning experiences and achievement of educational goals.

Everyone Loves an Experience: Turning worksheets into interactive activities or creating simulations and experiences where students actively engage with the content can yield profound results in education. Incorporating movement into learning activities has been shown to improve attention spans and enhance student engagement. By providing hands-on experiences and opportunities for students to immerse themselves in the subject matter, educators can effectively boost academic achievement and promote positive student behavior.

Engaging students in experiential learning not only keeps them actively involved, but also reduces the challenges of classroom management. When students are deeply engaged in meaningful activities, they are more likely to stay focused and participate enthusiastically, making teaching more enjoyable and effective. This approach not only enriches learning experiences but also supports educators in creating vibrant and dynamic classrooms where both learning and enjoyment thrive.

The Result

Disengaging instruction creates an environment in which disengaged students are more likely to make poor choices. This book is a testament to the transformative power of collaborative strategies in fostering dynamic classroom management. Student engagement directly impacts the overall atmosphere within a classroom. From in-depth projects to simple warmup activities, everything has a purpose.

> Disengaging instruction creates an environment in which disengaged students are more likely to make poor choices.

Icebreaker activities provide an opportunity for students to "jump right in," and become involved in class. I have always found the faster you can engage students in controlled discussions, cooperative learning, and the sharing of ideas, the more likely they are to continue that trend and feel a sense of connection to the class. Engaged students are more likely to participate positively, leading to a more cohesive and productive learning environment.

Examining your instructional practices through strategies such as the 3C's (Collaboration, Creativity, and Critical Thinking), project-based learning, student inquiry, creating classroom experiences, and engaging icebreaker activities can profoundly impact the learning environment and classroom management. These approaches foster an atmosphere where deeper learning occurs. Students engage critically with the content, laugh, smile, enjoy the learning process, and build meaningful relationships. This environment not only enhances academic achievement but also creates a positive and dynamic classroom culture.

Remember, your passion is contagious. When you're excited about teaching, students are more likely to be excited about learning. Keep things fresh, relevant, and interactive. You're not just teaching content; you're nurturing a love for learning that will extend beyond the classroom. Every small step towards engagement is a giant leap towards better classroom management and a more effective learning environment.

Your efforts can create an atmosphere where students are so invested in their education that behavior issues become a distant memory. Let's make your classroom a place where every student is tuned in and ready to learn. When that happens, classroom management is no longer the primary concern, and the passion that once drove you into this profession can steer your motivation and rekindle your spirit.

Let's Discuss

How can we, as educators, creatively integrate our students' diverse interests into our lesson plans to establish a more engaging and collaborative classroom environment, and what impact do you think this will have on the classroom management and student behavior?

CHAPTER 4

~

Meaningful Meetings: Be Intentional

"Turn an obligation into an advantage."

Crafting Collaborative Cultures: A Guide for Educators

As educators, we recognize that meetings are a valuable tool for the growth and advancement of our schools. They can be powerful venues for data analysis, instructional improvement, professional development, and fostering teacher relationships. Nonetheless, we also know that not all meetings are created equal—some can feel aimless and draining. The goal of this chapter is to discuss this concept, alter our perspective on the purpose of school meetings and revolutionize our implementation. Providing a framework for effective meetings and strategies for school-wide teacher collaboration can lead to innovation from within. By transforming every meeting from a perceived obligation into a dynamic, valuable tool for sharing effective instructional strategies and fostering school-wide collaboration, we can enhance our educational environment and drive continuous improvement.

Maximizing the Impact of Meetings

During a conversation with a pair of superintendents discussing the hot topic of taking things off the shoulders of teachers, my first recommendation was to eliminate meaningless meetings and, furthermore, make our meetings more purpose-driven. It is essential to point out that meetings are necessary for academic and school success and often contribute considerable value. Meetings are often an asset to drive our schools forward. For example, data is a valuable tool to help see where our students are and decide how to better address their needs through instruction. We can analyze how we are teaching and adjust accordingly. Meetings can provide great motivation, foster teacher relationships, facilitate professional development, and spark deep conversations about how to improve our teaching and student learning.

However, there are many cases where a meeting could have been an email. You know what I'm talking about—those meetings that happen, and we leave wondering what the purpose even was, or the meetings that seemingly last an eternity when they could have been short, sweet, and to the point. This goes beyond teachers, by the way. It's not a teacher thing or an administrator thing. It's an education thing. These are what I like to refer to as "meaningless meetings."

Teachers and administrators alike are overwhelmed with endless meetings that are often unproductive and tiring, which not only wears them out, but negatively affects students and undermines the positive school culture that has been established over time. The consequences of such nonstop meetings are more damaging than many might understand. The time is now to alter our lens on meetings because what can be done now could change the narrative and trajectory of your school.

An Innovative Approach

As educators, we have a decision to make: use our time to craft engaging lessons that spark joy and curiosity in our students or get bogged down in endless meetings that drain our energy and creativity. While it's not always our choice, when we prioritize planning time, we can create lessons that truly resonate with our students. Instructional planning leads to collaborative learning and interactive classrooms. This not only enriches our students' learning experience but also strengthens the bond between school and home as students share their enthusiasm for learning with their families. Often, the first parent-teacher conference comes from the voices of our students at home. What are they saying?

> Often, the first parent-teacher conference comes from the voices of our students at home. What are they saying?

It's time to take an innovative approach to our grade-level and school-wide meetings, transforming them from mere obligations into sessions of shared growth and genuine professional development. Together, we can build a thriving educational environment where everyone—students, teachers, and families—feels the positive impact.

From Obligation to Advantage: A Framework for Success

Just like the most engaging and effective lesson plans, school-wide meetings need to be well thought out and generated with authentic and relevant objectives. Our actions as a staff must be intentional. When we gather as a group, there must always be a specific focus. Rather than using meetings as a "time-suck" that wears down our staff, let's use them as purposeful opportunities to build community and come together to create something that works to our advantage.

There are so many amazing educators working in your school. Why aren't we using the great work that happens each day to our advantage? What if our grade-level, PLC, content, and staff meetings were designed with the purpose of creating, sharing, and learning from one another? Just think of the opportunity here. As the instructional coaches and administrative staff go into classrooms, enjoying moments with students and continuing to build community, they take note of the effective instructional strategies being used. We need to use those observations to help our staff become better together. This is where our meetings can become an advantage.

Once an engaging lesson is observed, we need to bring that greatness to the forefront for others to learn from and take note. Let's be honest, the best teachers are great at borrowing ideas and often improving them in the process, drawing inspiration and creativity from others. We can even use our grade level and PLC time to share and refine our ideas. Each month, we can allocate time for teachers to discuss at least one successful activity from their class and engage in a discussion about how it might be adapted for use in other classes.

The next step is for teachers to present their outstanding work. When a great activity is identified during a walk-through, a grade-level, or PLC meeting, we should encourage those teachers to provide a brief overview and share their successful lesson activities with their team and the entire staff. It doesn't need to be a lengthy explanation; a quick synopsis will suffice to maintain the attention and focus of the staff.

Each month, we can allocate time for teachers to discuss at least one successful activity from their class and engage in a discussion about how it might be adapted for use in other classes. By sharing these successes, a culture of collaboration and continuous improvement is fostered, and every one can benefit from the collective expertise and creativity of the staff.

To keep the focus and ensure the discussions are to the point, limit each presentation to three to five minutes tops. If the administrator or instructional coach has the opportunity, they should take a quick video clip or a few photos of the great work being done as a visual learning tool for the next staff meeting. Teachers and administrators can then dive deeper into conversations about what they liked and perhaps how they would modify or add to the lesson. This models the expectation of collaboration among peer teachers, much like how we model our classroom instruction with our students. In this way, real learning and staff development begin to take shape.

Another effective strategy is to have teachers engage in the actual activity. Turn a staff meeting into a ten-minute "Human Bingo" activity with prizes for the winning team where teachers can learn the "how" of individual activities while sharing smiles and laughs, and most importantly, learning from each other and building relationships together as a team. This approach transforms a seemingly meaningless meeting into one that is truly meaningful.

Focusing on instructional activities that are not grade-level or content-specific but adaptable to various grade levels or subject areas opens up endless possibilities. This can be an opportunity for teachers to share and discuss, creating real professional development built from the greatness within your own school. By taking things off the shoulders of the staff, cutting out the meaningless meetings, and holding meetings with a specific purpose, we can use our time as a continuous professional development opportunity for teachers to learn, share, and grow together.

A Forward Direction

Changing the narrative begins with taking action. Instead of looking elsewhere and wondering what makes other schools unique, we should believe in ourselves as a school community. Recognize that within our own districts and schools exists a wealth of talented teachers bursting with new ideas waiting to be shared. By harnessing the strengths and creativity within our own schools, we can leverage these assets to propel our schools and classrooms forward in a positive direction. In this way, we embrace and amplify the greatness that already exists in our own educational community to foster continuous improvement and success.

The next step is the development of a living document that serves as a repository for our collaborative efforts, continuously built upon year after year. This document is not static; it evolves with each meeting where instructional activities are shared and refined. The goal is to create a practical resource that supports teachers in assessing and implementing innovative teaching strategies without feeling overwhelmed. Unlike lengthy, exhaustive lesson plans, these documents will consist of concise synopses, supplemented with pictures or example documents for clarity. Keeping the content streamlined and accessible ensures that educators can easily navigate the document, find inspiration, adapt ideas, and integrate them into their own classroom with ease.

A Framework for Effective Meetings

Purpose-Driven Meetings: Ensure that every meeting has a clear objective aligned with educational goals, whether it's curriculum planning, sharing best practices, or professional development. This approach mirrors a teacher's lesson plan, where academic objectives are clearly defined to guide students through the day's activities. Similarly, a purpose-driven meeting states its objectives clearly to ensure that staff members understand the goals, fostering active participation and buy-in. Think of this like a teacher's lesson plan. The academic objectives for the day are clearly stated so students know what is expected and what the purpose of the class is each day. A purpose-driven meeting is the same with the objective clearly stated and understood so staff members understand the goals, which will encourage active participation and buy-in.

Data-Informed Discussions: Use student data as a foundation for discussions about instructional strategies and interventions. This includes providing insights into student engagement and its impact on academic achievement, as well as sharing research on how methods like movement, creativity, collaboration, project-based learning, and student inquiry can enhance learning outcomes and assessment results. This data-driven approach establishes that meetings are not only purposeful but also grounded in evidence-based practices that support continuous improvement in teaching and learning.

Time-Efficient Planning: Keep meetings concise, purposeful, and results-oriented. Whenever possible, opt to share information via email if it retains its value and doesn't necessitate a meeting. Ensure that meetings are held only when necessary, communicating to your staff that their time is highly valued. This approach helps maintain productivity and respects everyone's time commitments within the school community.

Peer-Led Professional Development: Empower educators to share their successful classroom strategies and innovations through concise, focused presentations. As school leaders observe lessons throughout the week, capture photos and videos of effective teaching practices. Request that these teachers provide a brief "how-to" synopsis of their lessons. Encourage teachers to share their engaging activities or fun ideas with the leadership team allowing for observation of the collection of visual materials like photos and videos. Consider using instructional coaches to compile these resources into a slideshow that includes detailed instructional activities, supplemented with photos and videos. This structured approach assures that presentations are well-prepared and effectively showcase the excellence within your school. By highlighting and supporting innovative practices, you can foster a culture of sharing and continuous improvement among educators.

Active Participation: Engage teachers in hands-on activities during meetings to demonstrate and practice new strategies. Incorporate a reflective period during which staff can openly share their thoughts, discuss what they liked, and brainstorm how they could adapt or implement specific strategies in their own classrooms. This approach not only reinforces learning through active participation but also encourages collaborative discussion and sharing of ideas among educators.

Continuous Improvement: Foster a culture in which feedback is embraced and collaboration is celebrated by implementing a school-specific system to capture and develop shared instructional strategies into a living document. Use a structured framework, as outlined in this book, to ensure consistency and clarity in documenting and sharing content. This approach creates easily accessible and understandable resources that support ongoing professional development throughout the school.

Shared Resources: Develop a living document or digital platform where educators can contribute and access all shared strategies, lesson plans, and resources. Once teachers share their lessons, the leadership team or instructional coaches can organize them and structure them in a way that aligns with the school's needs and standards. This process prevents burdening teachers with administrative tasks, beyond creating the initial blueprints. Instead, instructional coaches can use these resources to collaboratively build an archive of effective teaching strategies and resources that benefit the entire school community.

Respect for Time: Balance the necessity of meetings with respect for teachers' planning and personal time by prioritizing the quality of meetings over their quantity. Ensure that meetings are purposeful, focused, and directly contribute to the professional development and collaboration of educators. Make every effort to eliminate unnecessary meetings and prioritize clear communication through alternative means like emails or digital platforms when appropriate. This approach respects teachers' time for planning and personal growth while still fostering a collaborative and supportive school culture.

If You Build it, They Will Come

The most valuable support an administrator can provide is equipping teachers with resources for success. Establishing a shared living document of engaging lesson ideas empowers educators to draw inspiration and motivation, and secures the tools necessary to excel. Meetings should no longer be seen as checkbox obligations but as vital check-ins where we help each other thrive.

> Meetings should no longer be seen as checkbox obligations but as vital check-ins where we help each other thrive.

Meetings are now opportunities to co-create our in-house professional development collection—a book of ideas forged collaboratively as a team or staff. This approach avoids burdening teachers during their planning periods and instead leverages our collective time to build something impactful together.

As we look ahead to the future of education, it becomes increasingly clear that enhancing student engagement hinges on our ability to innovate how educators collaborate. School leaders must reimagine staff meetings, transforming them from routine obligations into dynamic professional development sessions marked by active collaboration. In doing so, we not only enrich teachers' professional lives but also create a ripple effect that positively impacts the classroom.

These collaborative meetings can serve as in-house workshops for instructional innovation, where educators share and refine practices that captivate and engage students. This is more than just a shift in meeting structures; it represents an educational transformation towards collective growth and student-centered achievement. As educators, we play a pivotal role in spearheading this evolution, ensuring that staff meetings become a cornerstone for educational excellence and continuous professional growth.

Let's Discuss

What specific changes could be implemented in staff meetings to directly influence instructional planning, encouraging more in-depth collaboration and dialogue among staff members? In what specific ways would these changes have a positive impact on instruction, student engagement, and school culture?

CHAPTER 5

~

Instructional Planning and School Collaboration

"We might teach twenty-five or thirty years, but we may only have these students for one. Let's make their learning unforgettable."

The Art of Lesson Plan Development for Educators

Zombies Attack! The moment zombies attacked my school, everything changed. One minute, I'm at my desk, ready to check my iPhone, and the next, I'm hitting record and sprinting full speed down the hallway. Lockers banged, and teachers stared as I flew around corners and downstairs, desperate for an exit. Outside, I found shelter behind a rundown trailer, once a classroom, now abandoned—an ideal spot to relay vital survival information.

Hysterically, I spoke into the camera, urging anyone who could hear to gather resources and reach the safe zone atop a city hospital before it was too late. Just as I was about to hit "end recording," the zombies approached at full speed. I took off running, only to trip, falling down a hill making a "thud" noise, my phone rolling and still recording.

I stood up, brushed the dirt and grass from my clothes, grinning and quite pleased with myself. I couldn't wait to see how my students would react.

Back in school, I quickly edited the footage in iMovie. Ten minutes later I had a black and white grainy horror-style two-minute movie with eerie background music, zombie screeches, and chilling eating sounds. It was all ready to introduce our new activity–zombies attacking our world!

The next day, the stage was set. As students approached my class-room, they were greeted by heaps of smashed, crinkled, and torn bul-letin board construction paper scattered outside my classroom door. Random strands of caution tape criss-crossed the hallway and a sign in red scratchy font read, "Zombie Apocalypse."

The feeling was eerie. My students entered a dimly lit room with my big screen set to play the opening video. Ominous music filled the room and the torn construction paper hanging from my ceiling tiles and covering the walls around my room, gave the illusion of a ravaged building. The students entered wide-eyed, their jaws hanging open in surprise and anticipation.

Accompanied by wide smiles and excitement, the questions came immediately. Soon, even students who were not in my class were drawn in by the sights and sounds, wanting to join in. Remarkably, the decorat-ing took little effort and cost basically nothing. Yet, this simple innova-tion set the tone and the energy in the room was palpable. My students' interest was not only piqued, it was also electric. Then I pushed play!

Students were on the edge of their seats about to be thrusted into the world of zombies, not yet realizing they were about to embark on a learning adventure. As you read this, you may wonder, "What could you possibly be doing with zombies that could get students to learn?" The answer: "Zombie Apocalypse Geography." In cooperative learning groups, students were about to use their geography skills and resources, including maps–typically a dry and sedentary activity–to work together.

They dove into the content, and quickly located resources to keep their team safe and navigate to the safe zone while fighting off the zombies trying to take over.

To be completely honest, I have never been a tech genius throughout my teaching career. For many years, the schools where I worked had inconsistent or unreliable technology so I didn't put much faith in its use, much less learn new apps and programs. Colleagues often laughed at my struggles—I was the "grandpa" of technology, fumbling to find the "on button" on my computer. For years, I stood in the same shoes you might find yourselves in today: hesitant and sometimes baffled by the rapid integration of technology in our classrooms. My journey began with a simple act: looking up "How to make a movie on my phone" online.

Even now, I won't claim to hold the answers to the digital challenges we face in education; however, with each small step, we improve together and our students benefit. It's from this place of uncertainty that I've experienced the most growth. Whether it's been banding together with colleagues to brainstorm or taking a moment to watch an online tutorial, these steps—small as they may seem—have sparked innovation in my lessons and enhanced student engagement in my classroom.

Consider my zombie attack scenario–a lesson plan that may seem complex at first glance, but was, in fact, born from modest beginnings. A quick internet search on video-making, a few minutes spent filming and editing, adding sound effects on a PowerPoint, and a concise narrative tied to assessment questions (now conveniently created with AI). This simple formula transformed a routine review into an unforgettable learning adventure for my students.

The inspiration to innovate often requires little more than the willingness to try, to stumble, and to explore. Each small effort is a step towards creating a memorable and engaging experience for our students. I encourage you to embrace the unfamiliar and reconsider how we design our instruction to make it more relevant, more authentic, and more engaging. Together, let's begin to look at building experiences our students will never forget.

Breakdown

Now that I have your unwavering attention, the essence of education transcends mere content delivery on a white board or reading from a text. It is about crafting an educational experience that ignites a fire of interest, passion, and drive deep within the hearts of our students. The aim of education and teaching isn't just to prepare students to pass tests; it's to build a continuous love of learning that extends far beyond the confines of our classrooms and school walls. It's about fostering an academic environment that empowers students to pursue their passions and nurtures a love for learning, providing them with the foundation to achieve their aspirations.

> The aim of education and teaching isn't just to prepare students to pass tests; it's to build a continuous love of learning that extends far beyond the confines of our classrooms and school walls.

It's easy to talk about creating engaging instructional experiences or turning worksheets into engaging activities, but the question remains: how do we achieve that? In my early years—and often to this day—I found myself grasping for creativity and new ideas. No classroom can be zombies and chaos all the time, no matter how seasoned a teacher is at lesson planning. There are times when students need to do sit-down work or guided reviews, but it is the engaging experiences and captivating activities that result in students working with an intense focus. They eagerly await the engaging activities. But again, how do we make this happen?

In this chapter we will delve into instructional planning, starting with unit plan set up to the development of detailed lesson plans. Reflective questions will be posed to spark thoughtful discussions about creating practical activities that lead to authentic learning experiences in our classrooms. By establishing a collaborative framework, we can build a collection of shared ideas to alleviate planning pressures on teachers. Through simple innovation and the creation of a living document of shared instructional activities we can draw inspiration, creativity, and freely borrow ideas from one another to make our everyday teaching life easier yet more effective for students.

Where to Begin

To create that foundational work we must first analyze what content knowledge we pour out and how we pour it out to ignite students to learn. Alongside dissecting our unit plans, content standards and objectives, essential questions, and instructional activities, it's crucial to adopt a reflective stance toward instruction. Instead of repeating the same methods annually, let's challenge ourselves to embrace new perspectives on our approach and the content we teach. Not to work harder or reinvent our teaching practices, but rather to simplify or modify what we already do in a practical way to make it more efficient and engaging.

As a father of two little girls, I honestly do not have the time I once had to develop the most insane instructional activities. That's not to say my lessons aren't effective and engaging, but I just do not have infinite hours to plan. I cannot spend hours on Pinterest or all my cash on Teachers Pay Teachers. I must be efficient with time management while also delivering meaningful and effective instruction. Like most educators, I don't have time to waste. As a father, I believe my daughters deserve the best possible education, so, as a teacher, I plan with the mindset of providing the kind of education to my students that I want my own children to experience. I believe the best education is found in a place where my students enjoy learning, want to come back to class, smile, laugh, and are deeply entrenched in authentic and relevant standards-based activities.

Being purposeful when planning is essential and I have been committed to mindfulness when crafting the lessons for my students. I carefully consider each instructional unit from the start, making sure that nothing is thrown together; everything is designed with my assessments in mind. While not every lesson is bursting with energy and innovation, I believe that even note cards and worksheets have academic purpose. I know that to run my class optimally, motivate my students, and fully enjoy my role as a teacher, I need to be well-prepared for each lesson when I step into my classroom.

The "What" vs. the "How"

The first step in unit plan development is understanding the content standards and student objectives while using a backward design method. This approach is not about teaching to a test but using the assessment as a valid and reliable tool to guide our instruction. Once we understand the direction of our teaching, we begin to devise a plan for content delivery. The standards themselves are the "what" behind the teaching, but the life we breathe into the lessons becomes the "how." Whether teaching fractions, cell development, counting coins, or the Constitutional Convention, how I decide to deliver that content is the game-changing ingredient. For this, I start by addressing the 3C's (collaboration, creativity, and critical thinking) of instructional development followed by powerful reflective questions to enhance the learning experience.

The 3 C's of Instructional Development

The 3 C's are an instructional development foundation to build from. Just like the foundation to a house or building project, if the foundation isn't right, the whole plan falls apart. Instructional planning is no different. If the foundation of our unit and lesson development isn't sound, the result will not be as effective as it could be. The 3C's, as mentioned in a previous chapter, consist of Collaboration, Creativity, and Critical Thinking.

Crafting activities that are authentic and relevant, requires examining the "WHAT" behind those activities. What are my students doing during the lesson? What do I want my students to accomplish in each activity? The goal is to produce engaging activities that get students collaborating and talking about the content, creating, or engineering something content-based. When this happens, students think critically and analyze the content in a much deeper way, resulting in higher-order thinking.

This can occur through project-based learning opportunities or student inquiry-based activities. In lessons where the 3 C's are the foundation, deeper learning and understanding takes place. Students are connected to the content and fully engaged, often without even realizing it.

Powerful Questions that Enhance Instructional Development

Another important step before creating our unit and lesson plans is to reflect on instructionally transformational questions. It is crucial to ignite the initial spark of inquiry even before the blueprint of our lesson takes form. The questions listed in this section can guide us towards creating lessons that resonate deeply with the lived experiences and authentic interests of our students.

How do I get my students up and moving? First, think about how to incorporate movement into your lessons. Whether it's a simulation of the human circulatory system, acting out a historical event, forming human math equations, or using activities like 4-Corners, the options are limitless. Imagine your students not just seated, but getting up, moving around, and having a blast while learning.

How do I get my students to create, build, or manipulate something? Envision each learner as a builder, engineer, artist, or creator. Reflect on how to provide tools for students to construct and shape their understanding in tangible forms. For a math concept, allow students to use formulas to design a city street, building, or roller-coaster with basic materials like cardboard and tape. Let them become engineers using math. Allow students to create a 3D wall timeline of story events or a lifelike science study guide that engulfs the classroom. They might paint a mural of historical events, build a rainforest model, or program a video game. Consider "Teaching to Learn," where students create a podcast or video as if teaching the next grade about a math concept, game rules in P.E., or a "Live from the Bottom of the Ocean" report in front of a greenscreen. Developing and writing an outline and script incorporates literacy and language arts skills. This approach helps students become teachers, changing how they process and retain knowledge. Imagine the collaboration, critical thinking, and active participation that results from these activities.

How can I incorporate a game or challenge? One of the best ways to enhance student engagement is through gamification. After completing guided math, lectures, or text analysis, amp it up. Take the "boring stuff" and make it fun with games like Grudge-Ball, Bluffing, Boom-Clap-Grab, or Splat Review. These strategies increase active participation and learning.

When attempting to enhance student engagement, educators should seek to incorporate students' interests such as TV shows, sports, video games, social media, or music. Infusing our curriculum with elements that resonate with students can transform a lesson from forgettable to impactful. Here are some ideas to get you started:

TV Shows/Movies/ Video Games: Connect themes from popular shows or movies to relevant topics. Use documentaries on platforms like Netflix to introduce or supplement material with real-world scenarios. For instance, when teaching physics, explain the science behind scenes in a popular sci-fi series. Create a gamified storyline, similar to a movie or video game experience, infused with review or essential content questions. Use AI apps to generate scripts and integrate questions within the storyline, making it easier to guide the lesson. Students can gain or lose points, shields, or resources based on their responses. Employ game-based learning where students explore historical events through simulations or solve puzzles requiring mathematical thinking.

Trends: Social media: Integrate platforms like TikTok by assigning students to create short educational videos to explain concepts. Integrate platforms like TikTok by assigning students to create short educational videos to explain concepts. They could develop a mock podcast or video cast to "be the teacher" and explain a mathematical concept or guide younger students through a textbook unit. This is not for posting on social media, but to use academic apps on school devices, infusing similar concepts for students to demonstrate content understanding.

Hobbies, Sports, Personal Interests: For a statistics lesson, analyze sports data to calculate probabilities or averages. Create a review game where student groups are football teams, and as they answer questions correctly, their team, represented by a helmet logo on a smartboard football field, moves ten yards. The team that scores the most touchdowns after a twenty-minute review wins the Super Bowl.

Music: In a language arts class, dissect song lyrics to study poetic devices or in a history class, explore different musical eras and their societal impact. Allow students to write a unit-in-review song or rap and record it as an assessment.

Books: Encourage creative writing by integrating AI-generated illustrations to bring stories to life. Take content understanding to the next level by incorporating storyboards, sketchnoting, or "create your own comic" activities to enhance comprehension and foster student creativity and choice.

Trending Topics: What's New: Keep up with the latest trends as they can enhance student-teacher relationships through conversations where students educate us. For instance, consider integrating new apps or viral challenges into educational activities. A trending dance could kick off a physical education class, explore rhythm in music, or serve as a warm-up or cool-down activity to foster relationships and enhance classroom culture, thereby boosting student engagement.

Remember, the key is to avoid forcing these interests awkwardly into lessons, but instead to discover genuine connections where students' natural curiosities align with the content learning objectives. This authentic approach not only enhances engagement but also illustrates the relevance of educational content to the real world, fostering a deeper connection to the material among students.

Look at what you've already done and ask yourself, "How can I improve this?" Reflective practice is a foundational aspect of lesson design, encouraging us to revisit and enhance our resources regularly in pursuit of educational excellence. For instance, transforming a traditional bingo worksheet into "Human Bingo" where students themselves become the bingo pieces on a floor-taped board can add an interactive twist. Similarly, a review worksheet could evolve into a gallery walk with questions posted around the room or a "Be the Teacher" activity where students critique your quiz answers. Another idea is to digitize hand-created assignments like sketchnotes using tools like Canva for a fresh look.

Additionally, using the "Four Corners" of your classroom for multiple-choice questions, assigning each corner as an answer choice, can engage students physically in answering questions. The goal is to build upon previous ideas to create something even better. By regularly asking ourselves, "How can I make this better?" we demonstrate our dedication to teaching and a growth mindset, enriching the educational journey of our students.

> Reflective practice is a foundational aspect of lesson design, encouraging us to revisit and enhance our resources regularly in pursuit of educational excellence.

How Can I Incorporate Technology and AI in Teaching?

As educators in a digital age, our instructional canvas grows ever more vibrant with the integration of technology and artificial intelligence, offering new avenues to enhance pedagogy and engage students in novel ways:

Digital Platforms: Embrace online learning environments such as learning management systems (LMS) to craft interactive and personalized learning experiences. These platforms can integrate multimedia content, collaborative tools, and facilitate communication among students and teachers.

Artificial Intelligence: Deploy AI-driven educational software that adapts to the learning pace and style of each student, providing tailored assistance and feedback.

Virtual and Augmented Reality: Incorporate VR and AR to create immersive experiences. Visualize complex scientific processes or historical events in a way that textbooks never could.

Data-Driven Insights: By harnessing the power of AI analytics, educators can create more adaptive and effective learning environments that cater to the diverse needs of students, fostering improved learning outcomes and educational experiences.

Automated Administrative Tasks: By leveraging AI tools to handle administrative tasks, educators can optimize their time, enhance instructional quality, and, ultimately, improve student outcomes through more personalized and engaging learning experiences.

Global Connectivity: Encourage global awareness and connectivity by using technology to partner with classrooms around the world for collaborative projects and cultural exchanges.

Creative Expression: Foster creativity through technology by empowering students to explore their interests to create digital art, music, or coding projects that showcase their understanding of a subject.

By integrating technology and AI into the mix of our instructional methods, we not only lead in educational innovation but also inspire our students to thrive in a tech-centric world.

Can I Turn a "WORKSHEET" into an "EXPERIENCE?"

Whenever possible, can I elevate this worksheet into an immersive experience for kids? Could you create a narrative or story around the worksheet content? Can students solve a mystery with math, or travel through history, encountering questions that shape the fate of civilizations? If it's a science worksheet on habitats, could students become different animals, advocating for their needs in a habitat council?

Gamify Learning: Can the worksheet be the basis for a game?

Absolutely! Transforming worksheets into immersive experiences not only makes learning more engaging but also fosters deeper understanding and retention of concepts. Here's how you can turn typical worksheets into dynamic learning adventures:

1. **Math Treasure Hunt:** Instead of solving math problems traditionally, create a treasure hunt where students must solve math problems to uncover clues leading to a hidden treasure. This adds excitement and motivation to math practice.
2. **Grammar Quest:** Turn a grammar worksheet into a quest where students embark on a journey to save a kingdom by correcting punctuation errors in sentences or paragraphs. Each correct answer moves them closer to completing their quest.
3. **Budgeting Simulation:** Transform a budgeting worksheet into a simulation where students manage a virtual small business. They make financial decisions, allocate resources, and analyze the outcomes to understand real-world applications of budgeting concepts.
4. **Collaborative Projects:** Instead of individual work, turn the worksheet into a collaborative project. Students can work in pairs or groups to solve problems, discuss strategies, and peer-teach concepts to each other. This promotes teamwork, communication, and deeper learning through shared understanding.

By infusing worksheets with narratives, simulations, and collaborative elements, educators can create memorable learning experiences that resonate with students. These approaches not only enhance engagement but also foster critical thinking, problem-solving skills, and application of knowledge in meaningful contexts. Transformative teaching goes beyond imparting information; it inspires students to actively participate, explore, and internalize learning, making education a dynamic and enriching journey.

Instructional Planning and Daily Implementation

The initial moments of a lesson are pivotal; setting the tone and direction for the learning is vital. As educators, how we introduce objectives and essential questions is crucial for engaging students from the start. I find it effective to keep it clear and straightforward. For example, I might say, "Today we are diving into _____. By the end of class, I want you to be able to explain these two key points, _____ and _____." This approach ensures transparency and sets clear expectations, allowing students to focus on learning with enthusiasm and purpose.

Here's why and how to start your lessons effectively once you've developed them:

Clarity and Transparency: Begin by clearly stating your lesson objectives in straightforward language. For example, say," Today, we're learning about the life cycle of butterflies. By the end of our class, I expect you to explain the four stages of metamorphosis and identify why each stage is critical to a butterfly's development." Keeping it direct assures students know the learning targets and expectations from the start. what the learning targets are and what your expectation is moving forward.

Connecting to Prior Knowledge: Activate students' existing knowledge by prompting them to recall related information. This primes their brains to connect new concepts to what they already know. Starting with a quick "verbal review" Q & A session from previous classes helps warm up their minds and reinforces learning.

Creating Relevance: Help students understand the significance of the day's objectives. When students grasp the "why" behind classroom activities, school rules, or classroom objectives, they are more likely to engage. Whenever possible, relate the lesson to their lives or current events to foster a sense of relevance. For example, explain how understanding the butterfly's life cycle mirrors roles in our community or compare solving math equations in peer groups to collaboration in business leadership.

Establishing a Safe Learning Environment: Assure students that it's normal not to know everything right away. Encourage questions and celebrate the learning process. "It's perfectly fine if you're not a butterfly expert yet—that's what we're here to explore and learn together."

By clearly stating the lesson goals and connecting them to engaging content, you demystify learning objectives and set clear expectations for student learning. This approach minimizes confusion, allowing students to approach the material calmly, ready to engage actively and purposefully. A clear and concise introduction followed by an engaging delivery results in students investing in the learning process, especially when they understand the relevance of what they're learning.

Setting the Stage: Captivating HOOKS for Memorable Experiences

Introducing objectives in an engaging manner is crucial to hooking your students' attention. Hooks come in many forms, captivating students from the onset. Perhaps show an intriguing video clip, post a shocking picture on your board, use props or lighting and music to set an "ambiance" that grabs students' attention.

For example, one effective hook I have used involved caution tape around my classroom door, an outline of a body on the floor, and a provocative question on the board: "Did Hitler really die or escape Europe during WWII?" As soon as students entered, their curiosity was piqued, and they were eager to dive into the day's content.

The hook serves as your opening act, creating a magnetic pull that draws students into the world of learning with curiosity and anticipation.

Making the Learning Engaging with Hooks

Visual Hooks: Imagine capturing students' attention by unveiling a startling image as they enter the room, sparking questions and curiosity about the day's topic. Whether it's a historic photograph, the use of props like caution tape or paper hanging from your ceiling, or a change in how desks are arranged, these changes can instantly pique student interest. Altering the classroom lighting or arrangement, can transport students into a different environment: soft dim lighting might introduce a lesson on deep-sea creatures, while arranging chairs in a circle can invite a discussion on literature. Setting an unusual tone to create an engaging atmosphere full of excitement.

Multimedia Hooks: Use a gripping video clip that aligns with the lesson's theme. A two-minute segment on environmental disasters can prompt students to brainstorm scientific solutions, or a suspenseful recording of an event ending like a cliffhanger from a movie trailer can leave students eager for more. The right footage can elevate the mood and transport students to different places and times or present a compelling problem that they'll be motivated to solve.

Auditory Hooks: Use music or a series of sounds to set the mood and atmosphere that captures the essence of the lesson. Music can evoke emotions and serve as a backdrop for a history lesson, while sound effects can bring a science concept to life. In my zombie apocalypse geography lesson, students entered a classroom with dim lighting and zombie groaning sounds with rain and wind sound effects from

YouTube. Before the lesson had a chance to begin, I had "hooked" student interest immediately.

Tangible Classroom Hooks: Introduce props that students can see and interact with the moment they walk in. Whether it's handling a model, examining a medical tool, or exploring a map, these tangible and out-of-the-ordinary hooks can grab the attention of the students and enhance engagement immediately.

Remember, the goal is to engage students' senses and emotions before a single instructional word is spoken. For instance, in a lesson on the *Triangle Shirtwaist Factory Fire*, I used burning sounds, dim lighting, and bulletin board paper torn hanging from my ceiling to generate the "feel" of a burned down building. The moment students walked in I heard questions such as, "What are we learning about today, Mr. A?" and comments such as, "It looks like the room burned down!" The hook not only starts the lesson but transforms the classroom into a space of intrigue and discovery.

Strategies for Teacher and School Collaboration

Collaborating and sharing our instructional development makes us all stronger. When we combine our knowledge and skills, we create a cohesive team that excels at solving problems and identifying new ways to enhance student engagement through our instruction. This isn't just about swapping lesson plans; it's about building a community where we support each other's growth. Whether it's discovering a new technological app to foster student creativity or sharing effective literacy or engineering strategies, collaboration fuels continuous improvement. Effective practices aren't one-time fixes but ongoing efforts that gather momentum, much like a snowball rolling down a hill. By maintaining a consistent focus on instructional development and courageously trying new strategies, we make our classrooms more exciting places to learn, advancing together as a team.

Focused Professional Learning Communities (PLCs): Use PLCs to delve into subject-specific strategies and share insights on student learning. This is where content teams can collaborate effectively and generate ideas to share across the entire staff. By leveraging our existing meeting times, we focus on creating together rather than adding more tasks. This approach continues to build a comprehensive school-wide resource of instructional plans, fostering a culture of collective improvement and shared knowledge.

Grade-Level Team Meetings: Coordinate grade-level meetings to discuss the development of content-area instructional strategies and identify cross-curricular opportunities. Share new resources and instructional practices across different subject areas, exploring how each can strengthen student learning. By drawing insights from each other, we enhance individual development while promoting collaborative efforts. This shared effort supports both horizontal alignment within subjects and vertical alignment across grade levels. For instance, consider collaborative efforts like integrating Math and Science or joint research assignments that utilize both English and History classes to enrich the learning experience for students.

Showcase and Share Sessions: Establish a regular routine for teachers to showcase effective instructional strategies, fostering peer learning and replication. Each session should feature a lesson title with concise instructions complemented by visuals such as pictures or videos to enhance understanding as the teacher presents to the group. Peers should observe and take note of potential ways to differentiate, modify, or creatively adapt the lesson for their content, grade-level, and student needs. This collaborative approach encourages the exchange of ideas and empowers educators to innovate within their own classrooms.

Collaborative Planning: Allocate dedicated time during meetings for teachers to co-create units or lesson plans, promoting a shared ownership and creativity. Recognize that each teacher's approach may vary to accommodate diverse student learning styles. This collaborative environment encourages the exchange of creative ideas among educators, aiming to cultivate excellence and eventually share innovative practices throughout the school.

Professional Growth Opportunities: Introduce a "spotlight" segment during meetings where teachers can showcase their professional readings, or innovative ideas that have influenced their teaching practices. This can be as simple as teachers sharing a cool idea they discovered on social media platforms such as Tik Tok or Instagram. By presenting short videos or visuals, teachers can feature practical classroom strategies that enhance student engagement and inspire others to implement.

Reflection and Feedback: Allocate dedicated time for teachers to reflect on recent initiatives or strategies and provide constructive feedback. This reflection can take place through mentorship sessions, grade-level meetings or whole-group staff meetings. The more we discuss and refine the use of new strategies together, the more effective and committed we will be to implementing the new ideas.

Celebration of Success: Acknowledge and celebrate successful implementation of shared strategies in the classroom. Introduce a spotlight success story segment during staff meetings where teachers can share instances when ideas from their colleagues enhanced student engagement. This positive reinforcement will strengthen the teaching community and amplify the greatness in your school. Encouraging teachers to share their successes inspires others to try new approaches, creating a ripple effect of innovation and improvement throughout the school community. Embrace these successes and continue to cultivate a culture where experimentation and growth are celebrated.

Administrative Support: Ensure that school leadership actively participates and supports these collaborative efforts, providing the necessary resources and backing. Engaging in the sharing process by contributing ideas, observations from classroom visits, and highlighting the successes of implemented strategies and their impact on student engagement. This involvement from leadership fosters a supportive environment that values collaboration and continuous improvement.

The Heart of Transformative Teaching

A fundamental truth is that if we aren't motivated to teach, our students won't be motivated to learn. Engagement starts with a plan. Great instruction doesn't just happen; it requires purposeful development, where we actively seek ways to create meaningful learning experiences. By providing avenues for student creativity, critical thinking, and collaboration and connecting content to student interests, we can enhance engagement. As we move forward, let's carry with us Maya Angelou's words with us: people will never forget how we made them feel. That sentiment lies at the heart of every lesson and every interaction we share with our colleagues and students.

Let's think back to the Zombie Attack lesson—an inventive plunge into geography that transported students into a thrilling, cooperative quest for survival. This lesson harnessed student interest and creativity, sparking excitement for learning. It shows that with a bit of ingenuity and the courage to try new ideas, we can turn even the most reluctant learners into enthusiastic participants in their own education.

Remember, innovation in teaching doesn't require us to be tech geniuses; it simply requires the heart to try and the spirit to explore. Let's keep collaborating, brainstorming, and building upon our ideas to create new learning experiences for our students. Every worksheet, every lesson plan, and every unit provides potential for something new and exciting. Embrace the unknown, welcome the unexpected, and remember: the journey of teaching is one of perpetual growth. It's about trying one new idea or changing one old lesson plan. It's progress over perfection, acting in small steps to improve our instruction and enhance the learning experiences our students will carry with them long after they leave our classrooms. The heart of transformative teaching is a willingness to try. We might teach for decades, but we may only have these students for one year. Let's make their learning unforgettable!

> Remember, innovation in teaching doesn't require us to be tech geniuses; it simply requires the heart to try and the spirit to explore.

Let's Discuss

As educators, we constantly seek to improve our lesson plans and activities to enhance student engagement. Reflect on a recent lesson that you taught. How could you redesign this lesson to better capture the interests and active participation of your students? Consider incorporating diverse instructional strategies, technology, and student-centered learning approaches in your redesign. Share specific examples and discuss the potential impact these changes might have on student engagement and learning outcomes.

CHAPTER 6

~

Amplifying Greatness: Action-Oriented Leadership in Education

"Change the status quo of instructional design."

Titles Don't Make Leaders. Actions Do!

Titles don't make leaders. Actions do, and great leaders lead by example and take action. Leadership is about building up those around you, amplifying the greatness of your teachers and school leaders, and providing pathways for greater success. It's about offering solutions and empowering others to find answers when you may not have them. Most importantly, a leader is not afraid to humble themselves, share the load, and get in the trenches with their staff to produce real transformative innovation.

In the chronicles of leadership, stories echo through time not just for their historical significance but for the timeless lessons they impart. One such story comes from the Revolutionary War. As the story goes, a military man on horseback came upon a group of soldiers struggling

71

to dig a defensive trench. Their superior officer, standing proudly above the trench, barked orders without lifting a finger to help. Seeing the men's fatigue, the soldier dismounted, seized a shovel, and toiled alongside the weary soldiers. When the superior officer protested, the man continued to help until the trench was complete, shoulder-to-shoulder with the other men. Once the work was done, he climbed up the walls of the trench and back onto his horse. He looked at the commanding officer and explained that the next time he was too proud to work alongside his men, he would be relieved of his post as an officer. At that moment, the once proud officer was humbled as he realized who the man on the horse was—George Washington. This act was not merely a display of camaraderie; it was a powerful lesson in leadership. Washington knew that titles do not inspire people; actions do. He understood that the measure of a leader is not found in the willingness to command but in the readiness to do what is necessary, to take action that uplifts and supports those you lead.

As school leaders, we often find ourselves in similar positions. We can choose to issue directives from a distance, or we can dismount from our positions and join our educators in the trenches. One key quality of great leadership is amplifying the greatness around you and helping others perform at their best. You can either play leader or be a leader—one who goes above and beyond for their teachers. A true leader provides resources, moves the needle, and pushes the school in a forward direction.

The greatness of our schools and the success of our students are amplified not just by what we instruct our teachers to do, but by what we are willing to do with them. One of the best things we can do as school leaders is provide the resources teachers and staff need to be successful and not be afraid to humble ourselves in the process. I love seeing school leaders grab the broom, fix the leaky water fountain in the upstairs hallway, or jump in and teach a class while teachers are sharing the load of substitute teaching when there aren't enough subs in the building. It is in the shared struggles and the collaborative efforts to dig through challenges that we truly lead and inspire.

In this chapter, we establish practical action steps to take and lead by example, providing an authentic look at strategies that impact instructional development and student engagement. These strategies allow school leaders to demonstrate their commitment to their staff and foster a collaborative, supportive environment.

First, as a school, define what student engagement means for you and develop a clear, shared understanding of what engagement looks like in practice, and create an initiative to generate a living document of shared resources throughout the school and district. This living document will revolutionize instructional planning and redefine how schools effectively collaborate. From the willingness to embrace the grind alongside your staff to the proactive approach of offering tangible solutions that teachers can use right now, these actions serve as a powerful catalyst for innovative change within our school divisions. Let us, like Washington, take a shared approach; for it is there, in the trenches of daily school life, that true leadership is forged and success is shared.

Being the Change: Implementing Action-Based Leadership

In the evolving landscape of education, the concept of leadership extends beyond administrative roles. Action-Based Leadership is a dynamic approach that requires educators to be at the forefront of change, taking a "lead from the front" approach to leadership. This involves innovating and transforming how education, and specifically student engagement, looks in your school. Additionally, Action-Based Leadership sets a standard for how schools can embody this model by actively engaging students and fostering a culture of shared learning and continuous improvement.

Student engagement is the cornerstone of effective teaching and learning. Before the development of a shared resource can happen, a school must first define what student engagement looks like within the context of their classrooms. Moving from compliance to critical thinking, student inquiry, and generating experiences in learning. This is not a static definition but an evolving one that reflects the needs and interests of students. Effective coaches don't make their players fit their game plan but rather establish a game plan that fits the skills and strengths of their players. They adapt to meet the needs just like educators do for their students.

As we delve deeper into this concept, I encourage you to reflect on your observations from the many classrooms you've experienced as both an observer and a teacher yourself. Consider these questions: What does student engagement look like? What does it feel like? What does it sound like?

Student engagement manifests in various forms. It can be seen when students are actively participating in discussions, eagerly exploring new concepts, and taking initiative in their learning journey. Whether it appears as organized chaos or quiet active learning, the key is that students are curious, motivated, and involved in their learning process.

As leaders, one of our primary responsibilities is to create pathways for our staff and students to achieve greater success. This includes providing opportunities for teachers to collaborate and develop authentic, practical strategies that enhance student engagement and can be shared across districts.

Crafting a Living Document of Shared Strategies

To capture the core of student engagement, schools can establish a "Living Document of Shared Strategies" aimed at enhancing student engagement, fostering enjoyable learning experiences, and alleviating the burden on teachers. This document goes beyond being a static repository of techniques; it evolves into a dynamic collection of authentic and pertinent instructional activities.

Year after year, this living document expands and adapts, offering increasingly comprehensive insights into how to effectively engage students in their learning journey. It serves as a collaborative resource where educators can continually contribute and refine strategies that resonate with students, ensuring that learning remains engaging and meaningful. Guidelines for the document:

Should Not Be Content or Grade Level Specific: Leadership should ensure that the strategies included in the shared resource are not limited to specific content areas or grade levels. It's essential to maintain a constant focus on universal applicability, allowing activities to be adaptable across different grade levels and subjects. Activities should be designed with scalability in mind, meaning they can be adjusted in difficulty and complexity. For instance, activities like "Human Bingo" can vary in question complexity depending on the age group and content area. This flexibility allows the same engaging strategy to be used effectively from Kindergarten through High School, making any class content enjoyable and interactive for students of all ages.

Easily Differentiated: Another primary focus should be ensuring that the strategies and activities shared are easily modifiable to accommodate diverse learning styles and the varying needs of students. While it may not be feasible to differentiate every activity for each content area or grade level, activities should be designed in a way that can be adapted for different learning levels. By incorporating flexibility into the design of instructional activities, educators can more effectively meet the needs of a diverse student population. This approach allows for adjustments in difficulty, complexity, or support mechanisms to ensure all students can engage meaningfully with the learning experience.

Collaboratively Built: A district-wide resource of shared strategies should be the culmination of collective wisdom and collaborative efforts, drawing from the experiences of all educators within the school division. Whether developed by a single school or through collaboration among multiple schools across the district, this approach should be viewed as an asset and an opportunity rather than an obligation. By pooling together insights, innovative practices, and successful strategies from diverse educational settings within the district, such a resource can effectively enhance teaching and learning outcomes.

Outsourcing Wisdom: Beyond the School Walls: Enhancing student engagement through a living document of shared teaching activities should transcend the boundaries of content areas, grade levels, or individual schools. It should embrace the concept of "outsourcing" ideas and strategies from educators across the district and beyond. This approach offers a new and innovative way to develop lesson plans, fostering true professional development through collaboration within and outside one's immediate environment.

By continuously outsourcing and collecting ideas from a diverse array of educators, the shared resource becomes enriched with a wide spectrum of strategies. This diversity ensures that educators have access to a broad range of effective teaching methods that can cater to various educational challenges and student needs. Moreover, extending the search to academic experts specializing in areas like gamification, technology integration, or literacy activities enhances the quality and relevance of the resources available to educators. Thus, promoting ongoing growth and improvement in instructional practices across the district.

Networking and Outsourcing for Knowledge: Building a network of educators who are willing to share their successful strategies is immensely valuable for fostering continuous improvement in teaching practices. The best educators recognize the value in borrowing ideas from their peers, and effective leaders understand the importance of leveraging outsourcing to gather and disseminate innovative strategies on a larger scale.

Every teacher, regardless of their experience level, possesses valuable insights and effective instructional strategies. Establishing an educator network dedicated to sharing these strategies within the district can be a powerful approach. This network should be cultivated through various channels, such as professional development sessions, collaborative meetings, online platforms, and informal discussions among educators.

By tapping into this network of experts in various academic fields, leaders can gather a diverse range of innovative strategies. This approach not only enriches the pool of teaching resources available but also respects the valuable time and expertise of the educators involved. It fosters a culture of collaboration and continuous learning, ultimately benefiting students by ensuring they receive high-quality instruction tailored to their diverse learning needs. This can be facilitated through:

Professional Learning Communities (PLCs): Use professional learning communities where regularly scheduled meetings already take place with teachers sharing insights and strategies. Start by collecting one high quality activity each quarter. Have your instructional coaches or teacher leaders model the expectation and take care of putting the resource together so you are not adding "another obligation" on the shoulders of your teachers. Rather, use this time for your staff to submit ideas to be included in the school-wide or district-wide document of shared instructional resources.

Use regular PLC meetings when teachers already gather to discuss curriculum, student progress, and instructional methods. This ensures that sharing insights and strategies becomes a natural part of their collaborative process. Empower instructional coaches or designated teacher leaders to facilitate this process. They can guide teachers on how to submit their ideas and compile them into a cohesive resource. This support helps streamline the creation of the school-wide or district-wide document of shared instructional resources. Emphasize that participating in this initiative should enhance, not detract from, teachers' existing responsibilities. Encourage teachers to view this as an opportunity to contribute and benefit from a collective pool of effective teaching practices. Ensure transparency and inclusivity by incorporating submitted ideas into the school-wide or district-wide document of shared instructional resources. This document should be easily accessible and regularly updated to reflect the evolving needs and innovations within the educational community.

Staff Meetings Become More Meaningful: Value the time of your teachers by defining the purpose of each staff meeting as a forum for sharing instructional strategies. Each teacher should leave the meeting with at least one new activity to implement in their classrooms. As a school leader, actively participate in these meetings by sharing your own ideas and examples of effective instruction you've observed. Collaborate with instructional coaches or administrators to create visual aids such as photos or videos taken during instructional rounds. These visuals should highlight effective teaching practices observed in the school or district. Allocate time during staff meetings for teachers to discuss these visuals. Encourage teachers to brainstorm how they can implement, modify, or adapt the activities shown to suit different grade levels or content areas. Capture the shared instructional activities discussed in meetings and add them to a structured template or document. This could be a school-wide or district-wide resource that continually evolves with new contributions, ensuring ongoing development and refinement of instructional resources available to teachers.

District-wide Workshops: Don't hesitate to organize district-wide workshops and events that enable teachers from different schools to showcase successful classroom practices. These events foster a sense of community and amplify excellence across schools, aiming to gather a diverse range of effective instructional strategies. Divide the workshops into focused areas that meet individual school needs, such as engaging activities for building classroom relationships and community, or integrating technologies like AI into content instruction. Encourage all educators to submit their finalized templates of ideas to a shared drive, ensuring consideration for inclusion in the district playbook of strategies to enhance student engagement. This proactive approach not only promotes collaboration but also ensures that best practices are shared widely, benefiting students across the district.

Online Forums and Social-Media: Harnessing technology and social media to establish platforms for outsourcing to instructional experts and expanding idea-sharing beyond our school walls marks a significant evolution. This approach elevates outsourcing and networking to new heights, facilitating connections among educators and introducing a modern approach to teacher coaching and collaboration. By connecting with educators nationwide, we cultivate a broader array of ideas and opportunities to engage instructional experts. This network can provide additional professional development through workshops and instructional coaching, enriching the expertise available to our staff.

A Tangible Approach to Supporting Teachers

For teachers to embrace and implement these strategies, the approach must be tangible and accessible. This means:

Practical Professional Development: Focused training sessions on specific needs to not only discuss, but also model, the strategies gathered. Making sure that our teachers walk away with practical ideas that can be implemented right away. Teachers want to see instructional strategies that work, and they want to see how they can be implemented right away.

Mentorship Programs: Pairing experienced teachers with newcomers to guide them in applying these strategies is key. Giving ideas is one thing but making sure that teachers who need help with student engagement are working with teachers whose strength is student engagement. We cannot just provide ideas and walk away, rather, we provide strategies and continue to focus on their implementation. These implementation and reflective conversations can also take place on a large scale during our PLC's and staff meetings.

Resource Allocation: It's crucial to ensure that teachers have the essential materials and technology to implement new ideas. Effective leaders prioritize understanding what staff members need for success. As we pursue a transformative approach to innovation through outsourcing and gathering new instructional ideas, it's imperative to provide teachers with the necessary resources to foster classroom innovation.

Recognition and Encouragement: Similar to how we celebrate the academic growth of our students, we must also celebrate the successes, both large and small, of our staff as they evolve as educators. By celebrating achievements and learning from setbacks, we cultivate a supportive environment that encourages instructional risk-taking. When teachers see that the instructional resource guide and strategies are actively used and celebrated, it inspires others to try new approaches. Let's ensure our ideas lead to a dynamic instructional revolution marked by shared successes and active participation.

Leadership in Action

Action-Based Leadership takes a proactive stance towards change, emphasizing student engagement through the creation of a shared resource of strategies. By enhancing the learning experience for students, we also empower teachers to innovate and respond effectively as educators. This collaborative and dynamic process positions our school to excel in education, setting a standard from the top down.

David Kohler's story, as recounted by Kenny Smith, former NBA player and sports analyst, serves as a compelling example of how humility can lead to informed leadership. Smith recalled his college days as summer roommates with David Kohler, heir to the Kohler plumbing empire. Despite his privileged position, Kohler insisted on starting at the bottom to work his way up through the ranks. His rationale was clear: to sustain the company's success, he needed a comprehensive understanding of every role within it.

This philosophy resonates deeply with educational leadership, emphasizing the importance of experiencing every layer of the system we aim to improve. Just as teachers should recall their student days, school leaders must remember the challenges of teaching to remain connected to the classroom and the educational community they serve. By understanding the anxieties and difficulties associated with lesson planning and instructional development, we can actively contribute to solutions that foster collaboration, outsourcing, and innovative change from within. This approach represents true professional development from within our own educational community.

In the journey toward educational greatness, akin to George Washington's leadership in the trenches and David Kohler's rise through the ranks, we see examples of action-oriented leadership. As educational leaders, our role extends beyond administrative duties to alleviating the stress of instructional planning through shared responsibility. By amplifying greatness within our walls through innovative change, we foster community across our school divisions. Together, we no longer seek solutions in isolation but build bridges of transformative action collaboratively.

The creation of our living document of collaborative instructional resources signifies a collective commitment to student success and underscores the power of unity in our educational journey toward academic achievement. Let's persevere in being agents of change, leading by example and embracing action-based leadership that will elevate our schools and redefine the status quo of instructional design.

Let's Discuss

How can we effectively "outsource" wisdom from beyond our school walls to enhance our instructional strategies and encourage continuous professional development and how we can use staff meetings and PLCs more effectively to gather and share innovative teaching strategies without adding to the workload of our teachers?

CHAPTER 7

~

The Framework, Lesson Template, and Ideas to Share

Within the dynamic world of education, a living document of collaborative shared instructional strategies serves as a collective of wisdom and creativity established from the experience and expertise of the educators across your school campus and division. This framework has been designed to evolve, celebrating the effective approaches and diverse evolution of teaching. The collection of activity resources and strategies shared here are those which I developed and gathered over my career as a classroom teacher working individually and with colleagues. Such shared resources have been modified and adapted in over the years in several ways to fit the needs and diverse academic backgrounds of my students.

As you read through, reflect on how you, your school, and district could modify both my template and the lesson activities shared to best fit the needs of your student populations. The best teachers use the knowledge and expertise of others, reflect on best practices, and differentiate and adapt ideas. Drawing from the creativity here is an excellent starting point to begin trying activities found here and drawing creative changes you might implement to generate even better ideas or ways to implement the following learning strategies.

Lesson Plan Breakdown

As you read through the following forty-five lesson activities, you will see a common theme in the set-up process. For each lesson you will see an objective with a basic overview. Just as a teacher would post an objective for students to understand the goal of the lesson, the activities here follow that same idea. Additionally, you will find materials needed along with a more in-depth activity overview, set up instructions, rules of the activity or game, and variations of each activity. Always consider how you can modify or create a new variation of these activities to fit the needs of your diverse learners. Finally, I have added other elements depending on the activity like things to consider and ideas for assessment of the activities. As with any lesson idea, it is always important to consider your classroom and student needs along with lesson plan setup modification demands based on your individual school needs. The best teachers borrow ideas and make them their own. So borrow,

modify, and use the following to enhance the learning experience for your students and the joy of teaching for yourself!

Relationship/Community Building Activities

Sample Lesson Activity: Head, Shoulders, Knees, COLOR!

Objective:
Students will participate in a kinetic and engaging activity called "Head, Shoulders, Knees, COLOR!" This exciting strategy encourages quick thinking, reflexes, and teamwork. This activity aims to inject energy

into the class, build relationships, and establish a community atmosphere, all while reinforcing color recognition for young kids and the concept of following sequential instructions.

Used for any level, this activity can start off the class as a warm-up, cool-down, start of the year, after a long break, or a fun Friday activity. Length can vary, but often 5-15 mins.

Materials:

+ Color markers (blue, green, red for each group – or other colors if they are consistent across groups)
+ Space in the classroom for students to move around freely. Typically, tables or put desks together.

Activity Overview:

"Head, Shoulders, Knees, COLOR!" is a lively activity inspired by the well-known children's song "Head, Shoulders, Knees, and Toes," but with an added twist involving colors and a point system. Students respond to commands called out by the teacher by touching their head, shoulders, or knees, and then quickly grabbing the color marker called out. An example, "Head, shoulders, head, head, knees, shoulders, knees, knees, BLUE!" This activity gets students moving, laughing, and engaging with each other, making it an excellent choice for a warm-up, brain break, or a relationship-building exercise at the start of the year or after a holiday break.

Setup Instructions:

1. Divide students into pairs or small groups, providing each group with a set of three-color markers. Add colors depending on your group sizing and student age.
2. Ensure there is enough space for each group to stand in a circle around the desks with markers without being too close to others, to prevent collisions.

Rules of the Game:

1. The teacher calls out "head," "shoulders," or "knees," and students must touch the corresponding body part.
2. The teacher will quickly switch between calling out body parts to keep students' alert.
3. Without warning, the teacher will shout out a color (e.g., "BLUE!").
4. The first student to grab the marker of the called color earns a point.
5. Play continues for 5-15 minutes, or as time allows.

Game Variations:

+ Solo play where each student has their set of markers. Use this as practice or for points—students lose a point if they grab the wrong color. Solo practice is more for younger ages as it will be less competitive.
+ Larger groups of 4 or 5 to increase difficulty.
+ Adding more colors to increase difficulty.
+ Integrating subject-related terms and content (e.g., "nucleus" for a science class, where students must grab the yellow marker or note card with a term or answer).

Skill-Building and Time-Limited Challenge:

+ Before starting the main activity, allow students a practice round to get used to the commands and the speed of the game.
+ Introduce a time-limited challenge where students must accumulate a certain number of points within the allotted time.

Scoring and Competition:

+ Keep a tally of points earned by each group.
+ Celebrate the group with the highest score or who played together with the best attitude even if they lost at the end of

the game, perhaps with a simple reward like a homework pass or extra recess time.

Closure:
Wrap up the activity by discussing what strategies worked best, how students communicated during the game, and the importance of being attentive and responsive. Celebrate good behavior and reward the whole class as a show of what class can be like if we play games and challenges the right way. Use this as an opportunity to draw parallels between the game and classroom dynamics, emphasizing that the classroom can be a space of fun and learning, and how their engagement is key to making that happen.

Assessment:
Evaluate students based on participation, enthusiasm, ability to follow instructions quickly, and teamwork during the activity.

Sample Lesson Activity: Tower of Terror

My day one, week one, or random Friday to build relationships, have fun, and create an inclusive classroom culture activity is called "Tower of Terror," named after the Disney theme park ride because of their similarity. If played correctly, it brings out an energy and the kind of positive environment that pulls students in. This activity also gets students smiling, laughing, and fully engaged, often asking, "Can we do this again tomorrow?" The best part is you can modify this kind of activity for any age and grade level.

Objective:
Students will participate in the following relationship building activity called "Tower of Terror" which encourages teamwork, strategy, and fine motor skills. This activity is designed to energize the class and foster a positive competitive spirit.

Materials:
- Plastic cups (enough to create stacks 3-4 cups high for each group)
- Sturdy large notecards (one for each gap in the cup stacks)

Activity Overview:
"Tower of Terror" is an engaging activity that can be adapted for any age group. It simulates the excitement and suspense of the Disney theme park ride with the same name and a similar outcome. The goal is to carefully pull notecards from between stacked cups without causing the tower to fall. Each successful attempt getting all cups in the stack to drop together results in a point for the group. I add points of all groups in each class together during each round to generate a total. Round times are three minutes each. With classes working together to beat the total score of my other classes now we are creating a "team" or "family" component to the activity. Working together to beat other classes' scores rather than competing against each other and causing division.

Setup Instructions:
1. Stack the plastic cups 3-4 high, inserting a notecard between each cup.
2. Ensure notecards are strong and not cut pieces of paper for stability.

Rules of the Game:
1. Players will take turns pulling out one notecard each or they can pull on the "count of 3" but each player pulls a different card.
2. If pulling a notecard causes the cups to fall sideways, the player responsible is "out" if it is a 1-on-1 game. If it is a group game, they just restack the cups as quickly as possible and continue playing until the timed round ends.

3. If the cups drop but remain stacked the team or individual earns 1 point.

4. The objective is to remove all notecards so that the cups collapse straight down together.

Game Variations:
+ Student vs. Student
+ Student vs. Teacher
+ Group vs. Group
+ Whole class vs. Teacher
+ Whole class vs. Whole Class (ex. Period 1 vs. Period 3) (Variation) Tournament Play:
+ Form groups of 4-6; one student from each group advances after each round.
+ Hold a championship round with the final two students.

Skill-Building and Time-Limited Challenge:
+ Allow students time to practice becoming familiar with the game and how to successfully get the cups to drop.
+ Introduce a time-limited challenge where groups must reach a set goal within 3-5 minutes.

Scoring and Competition:
+ Keep a cumulative score for the class as they work in groups. Ask groups to call for your attention so you see the cups successfully dropped each time to raise the energy level in the class and to keep an accurate continuous score.
+ Announce the time and maintain the pace as students attempt to beat the score of the day.
+ Create a class leaderboard to foster healthy competition between classes. This is a great way to keep kids energized during the activity. Playing upbeat music also helps.

Closure:

Conclude the activity with a discussion on strategies used, reflections on teamwork, and observations about the energy and positive collaboration between students. Use this as a moment to mention how learning and class can be fun but that depends on how students react to each other and to the learning environment. If we can be respectful and show, we want to have fun activities like this while learning content will continue. Be sure to explain that learning can be engaging and fun or boring and students' reactions, responses to each other, and actions during these games will determine the activities you decide to use throughout the year.

Assessment:

Evaluate students on participation, teamwork, and the ability to strategize effectively during the game.

Sample Lesson Activity: The Almost Impossible Cup Pyramid

Objective:

Students will engage in a team-building exercise that challenges their collaboration, cooperation, and problem-solving skills. The activity requires groups to construct various pyramid structures using red solo plastic cups, with the ultimate challenge of building "The almost impossible pyramid."

Materials:
- Six red plastic solo cups per group
- One rubber band large enough to fit around the cups per group.
- One piece of yarn (8-12 inches long) per student. I like to use yarn rather than string because yarn is easier to hold and less likely to rip the rubber band during the activity.

90

Activity Overview:
The Impossible Cup Pyramid is a collaborative relationship and team building activity that tests students' ability to work together to manipulate objects using indirect methods. The task is to construct a series of pyramid structures made up of red plastic solo cups as first demonstrated by the teacher, culminating in an advanced structure of cups deemed "the almost impossible pyramid."

Setup Instructions:
1. Form groups of four or five students.
2. Distribute six cups, one rubber band, and one piece of yarn per student to each group.

Rules of the Game:
1. Each student ties their piece of yarn to the rubber band, spacing the yarn evenly around it.
2. Each student must have only one piece of yarn but can trade at any time to aid in moving the cups or successfully building the pyramid.
3. Students can only hold their piece of yarn and are not allowed to touch the cups directly with their hands or any part of their body.
4. Movement, trading yarn, and strategizing are allowed, as long as students do not touch the cups with their bodies.
5. If the cups fall, students can only then pick them up to restack and start over. To allow for greater success and activity buy-in I allow a dropped or fallen cup to be returned to the stack but not restack all the cups.
6. The initial goal is to deconstruct a stack of cups and arrange them into a pyramid shape.

Pyramid Challenges:

- Start with a basic pyramid structure of three cups at the base, two in the middle, and one on top.
- Progress to a layer of three upright cups, with three inverted cups balanced on top.
- Introduce more complex pyramids, leading up to "the almost impossible pyramid" where all six cups are stacked vertically, one on top of the other.

Closure:

Discuss the challenges faced, the importance of communication, and the strategies that led to successful pyramid construction.

Assessment:

Evaluate the groups on their ability to work cohesively, their strategy development, positive collaboration, and their success in constructing the pyramid structures as the rounds progressed and the pyramids became progressively more difficult.

Sample Lesson Activity: The Scribe

Objective:

Students will engage in a collaborative activity designed to foster communication, cooperation, and fine motor skills. "The Scribe" requires students to work together to write or draw with a marker controlled by yarn attached to a dry erase marker using painters' tape.

Materials:

- One piece of painters' tape about 6-8 inches long (I like painters' tape because it's easier to use and sturdier)
- One piece of yarn (8-12 inches long) per student
- One dry erase marker per group

- Something to write and draw on (large paper, desk, or whiteboard)

Activity Overview:
In "The Scribe," students are tasked with writing or drawing on a desk, large paper, or whiteboard using a dry erase marker that is manipulated indirectly through yarn attached by tape. The activity emphasizes teamwork and the development of interpersonal relationships and both verbal and non-verbal collaboration.

Setup Instructions:
1. Organize students into groups.
2. Provide each group with tape, a piece of yarn for each student, and a dry-erase marker.
3. Have students tie or connect their yarn to the dry-erase marker in any way they wish, distributing the yarn with enough slack to be used but not physically touching the marker.

Rules of the Game:
1. The dry erase marker is placed standing upright on the desk.
2. Students must only hold their piece of yarn and cannot touch the marker directly with their hands or any part of their body once it has been taped and the activity has begun.
3. The group must work together to move the marker and write or draw the assigned task.
4. If the marker falls, students can reset it upright.
5. The goal is for the group to use the marker to write a number, word, or draw a simple picture as assigned by the teacher.
6. To advance the difficulty level during a given round, do not allow verbal communication. Finally, student depending, for the most difficult round allow verbal communication but eyes must be closed, and students must talk it out.

Task Examples:

- ◆ Write a specific number or series of numbers.
- ◆ Write a word or a short sentence.
- ◆ Draw a simple picture, such as a snowman.

Closure:

Conclude with a group discussion about the strategies that were effective, the challenges of working together, and the importance of communication in collaborative tasks.

Assessment:

Evaluate student groups based on their ability to collaborate, communicate, and successfully complete the writing or drawing task.

Sample Lesson Activity: Face-Off

Objective:

Students will participate in an interactive game called "Face-Off," which reinforces math skills such as addition, subtraction, or multiplication, and promotes relationship and community building. The game is designed to create a lively and collaborative atmosphere, encouraging students to interact positively and enjoyably in a structured setting.

Materials:

- ◆ Space for pairs or small groups to stand back-to-back.
- ◆ Optional: flashcards with numbers for younger students or those who need visual support

Activity Overview:

"Face-Off" is a speed game where students in pairs or small groups face away from each other and on cue, turn around to quickly solve a math problem or simply engage in a playful competition. This activity allows students to get on their feet, share laughter, and work together, serving both educational and social development purposes. It can be adapted to various mathematical operations (such as addition, subtraction, or multiplication) and is a great way to warm up for a class, take a quick fun brain-break, or integrate into a lesson for active learning.

Setup Instructions:
1. Have students pair up or form small groups, standing back-to-back with a bit of space between them.
2. Students place one hand on their heart with a few fingers held out to show a number from 1-5.

Rules of the Game:
1. On the teacher's countdown, students turn to face each other and simultaneously show their chosen number of fingers.
2. The first student to correctly add, subtract, or multiply the numbers aloud wins the round and earns a point.
3. For example, if one student shows 3 fingers and the other shows 5, the first to say "8" wins for addition. You can do the same with subtraction or multiplication or add both hands to raise the difficulty level for older students.
4. Continue for several rounds, adjusting the time based on engagement and the flow of the class.

Game Variations:
+ Utilize subtraction or multiplication for different rounds.
+ Have students use both hands to increase the range of numbers and difficulty.
+ Implement bracket scoring or timed challenges (e.g., "most points in 3 minutes").
+ The winners from each group can compete in a final round against the teacher for added fun.

Skill-Building and Time-Limited Challenge:
- Allow students to practice their math skills in a low-pressure environment before the game begins.
- Introduce a version of the game that is timed to increase the competitive element and focus.

Scoring and Competition:
- Keep track of points for each student or group.
- Encourage friendly competition with a lighthearted approach to winning and losing.

Closure:
End the activity with a class discussion on the strategies used, the cooperation observed, and the importance of teamwork. Emphasize the connection between positive behavior and fun classroom activities. Highlight the value of engagement and respect in creating a fun learning environment and promise to continue incorporating such activities as long as the positive atmosphere is maintained. Challenge students to go home and teach the activity and play with family members or other friends.

Assessment:
Observational assessment of students based on active participation, the ability to quickly solve math problems, cooperation with partners or group members, and the demonstration of good sportsmanship and positive behavior during the activity.

Sample Lesson Activity: Puzzle Maker

Objective:
Students will engage in a collaborative activity called "Puzzle Maker" to enhance engagement, foster teamwork, and build community within the classroom. By working together to assemble a large-scale puzzle,

students will exercise their problem-solving skills and ability to work cooperatively.

Materials:
- A large image printed or drawn on butcher paper or bulletin board paper.
- Scissors or a paper cutter to create individual puzzle pieces.
- Optional: Laminator to reinforce paper pieces if the puzzle will be reused.

Activity Overview:
"Puzzle Maker" is a hands-on activity where students put together a large puzzle that has been divided into pieces. Each student or small group is responsible for a piece of the puzzle, and together they must figure out how to assemble the complete image. This activity can be content-neutral, simply for community building, or content-specific by using images related to curriculum topics. It's an excellent tool for teaching collaboration and the collective achievement of goals.

Setup Instructions:
1. Select a large image appropriate for the class size and educational purpose and print or draw this image onto a large sheet of paper. Create more than one if you split students into smaller peer groupings.
2. Cut the image into pieces that correspond to the number of students or groups in the class.
3. Shuffle the pieces to mix them up before distribution.
4. Hand out one piece per student or per small group.

Rules of the Game:
1. Students receive one puzzle piece each (or each group receives multiple pieces for larger group puzzles).

2. The task is to figure out how their piece fits into the larger picture, without knowing what the final image looks like.

3. Students can trade pieces with others if they believe it will help complete the picture.

4. The goal is for the class to work together to assemble the puzzle correctly on a large flat surface.

5. Organize an additional 2nd round without verbal communication to increase difficulty for older age groups once students understand the objective.

Game Variations:

+ Content-specific puzzles that relate to a unit of study, such as historical events, biological diagrams, or literary themes.
+ Time challenges for assembling the puzzle to add a competitive edge.
+ Small group competitions where each group has a puzzle to assemble and the first group to complete it correctly wins.

Skill-Building and Time-Limited Challenge:

+ Introduce elements of the current curriculum into the puzzle to make the activity a learning experience.
+ Allow students time to strategize and plan their approach before beginning the assembly.

Scoring and Competition:

+ While this activity is more about collaboration than competition, consider acknowledging the group that first correctly assembles their puzzle or offers a reward for best cooperative group or the whole class once the puzzle is completed.

Closure:

Conclude the activity by reflecting on the collaborative process, the strategies employed by students, and the benefits of working together toward a common goal. Reinforce the idea that each student's contribution is vital to the completion of the whole and that this mirrors the importance of every individual's role in the classroom community.

Assessment:

Evaluate students on their participation, communication with peers, problem- solving strategies, and ability to work collaboratively. Consider the group dynamics and how students negotiate roles and share tasks during the activity.

Instructional Content Strategies

Sample Lesson Activity: The Quiet Debate

Objective:

Students will take part in a silent, written discussion known as "The Quiet Debate." This activity aims to engage students in critical thinking, problem-solving, debating, and literacy by exploring essential questions or statements related to content areas in a non-verbal format. The goal is to provide an inclusive environment where all students can confidently express their thoughts and ideas.

Materials:

+ Poster paper or large sheets of anchor chart paper posted around the room.
+ Markers or pens for students to write their responses.
+ A list of essential questions or open-ended statements related to the current unit of study written in large font at the top of the anchor chart paper.

Activity Overview:

"The Quiet Debate" is an activity where students communicate in writing in response to critical questions or statements without speaking until the end of the session. This method encourages thoughtful reflection and allows students who may be reluctant to speak in public to engage deeply with the material. It can also serve to highlight diverse perspectives within the classroom on content-related issues.

Setup Instructions:
1. Post essential questions or open-ended content-related statements around the classroom.
2. Provide markers or pens for students to write with.
3. Explain the rules to the students, emphasizing the no-talking rule until the end. This activity can take as short or as long as the teacher wishes. Typical timeframe is ten minutes plus to give students time to think and write.

Rules of the Activity:
1. Students silently walk around the room reading the posted questions and statements.
2. They can write a response, pose a new question, answer someone else's question, or comment on another student's response.
3. Encourage students to build on each other's ideas by elaborating on existing responses.
4. Maintain a quiet environment to allow students to focus on their thoughts and the written dialogue.
5. Occasionally comment on some good dialogue you notice to promote more of the same from other students who may need a "nudge" on what and how to write.

Game Variations:
+ After the silent debate, have a written reflection where students answer the essential question using what they've learned from their peers' responses as evidence.

- Rotate groups of students through different questions or statements in timed intervals to structure the activity.

Skill-Building and Time-Limited Challenge:
- Allow students to practice writing succinct, clear arguments or questions to contribute to the debate.
- Consider setting a time limit for each student at each station to ensure all can contribute to multiple questions or statements.

Closure:
After the silent writing period, transition to a whole-group discussion to vocalize thoughts and reflections on the activity. Discuss how this silent format allowed for different kinds of participation and whether it changed the nature of the debate compared to a traditional verbal discussion.

Assessment:
Assess students on their engagement with the activity, the quality of their written contributions, their ability to build upon other's ideas, and their participation in the concluding discussion. Evaluate their understanding of the content as well as their critical thinking skills displayed through their written responses and post-activity reflective responses.

Sample Lesson Activity: 3D Wall Timeline

Objective:
Students will create a "3D Wall Timeline" that visually sequences information from a variety of subjects. This activity encourages students to analyze content, arrange information chronologically or logically, and work collaboratively. It can be tailored to any subject area, such as organizing the stages of cell division in science, outlining key events

in a historical period in social studies, or plotting the development of a character or events in a story for English class. Another modification would be to have students create a 3D Wall Summary of a unit or a visual representation of a study guide for the upcoming test. "SHOW ME" what it looks like and provide the necessary vocabulary or information and teach me what I need to know.

Materials:
+ Large sheets of anchor chart paper or butcher paper for creating timelines.
+ Markers, post-it notes, index cards, construction paper, and other stationery materials for creating and writing events or information.
+ Tape or magnets for attaching materials to the wall.
+ Textbooks, computer research, novels, or content source materials for reference.

Activity Overview:
The "3D Wall Timeline" is a hands-on group activity where students work together to create a large visual representation of sequenced information on a classroom wall. By physically arranging and connecting pieces of information, students gain a deeper understanding of the relationships and progression within the content. The activity is adaptable to different grade levels and subjects by varying the complexity of the tasks.

Setup Instructions:
1. Assign each student group a section of wall space or decide on a single large wall for the whole class to use.
2. Provide each group with the materials needed to construct their section of the timeline.

3. Offer guidelines on the scope and sequence of the content to be included.

Rules of the Activity:
1. Students work in groups to sequence information on their wall space according to the assigned content.
2. Each piece of information added to the timeline should be connected logically or chronologically to others.
3. Groups can add depth to their timelines with drawings, quotes, or 3D elements that pop off the wall to create a more engaging visual effect.
4. Encourage students to discuss and debate the placement of information to ensure accuracy and comprehension.

Activity Variations:
- For younger students, use pictures and simple terms.
- For older students, incorporate primary sources, direct quotations, and more complex analysis.
- Allow students to use technology to print out or design elements of the timeline.
- Consider using an AI image generator app to have an unlimited source of image options. This will enhance student engagement and creativity on this assignment. Now nothing is off the table in how students develop their assigned section or content.
- Additional modification-have students create a 3D Wall Summary of a unit chapter in the textbook or a visual representation of a study guide for the upcoming test. "SHOW ME" what it looks like and provide the necessary vocabulary or information and teach me what I need to know.

Skill-Building and Time-Limited Challenge:
- Provide a set amount of class time for groups to work, fostering focus and efficient teamwork.
- Allow students time to research and outline to verify the correct sequence before starting the timeline.

Closure:

After completion, hold a class discussion where each group can explain their section of the timeline. Discuss the importance of sequence and cause-effect relationships within the subject matter where appropriate. Connect the activity to broader learning objectives and skills such as analysis, synthesis, and collaborative learning.

Assessment:

Evaluate groups on the accuracy of their sequencing, the completeness of the information, and the creativity of their presentation. Consider individual contributions to group work, communication among group members, and the ability to justify the placement of information on the timeline.

Sample Lesson Activity: 3D Math Wall

Objective:

In this math-focused adaptation of the "3D Wall Timeline," student groups will work collaboratively to solve math problems posted around the classroom. This lesson, titled "3D Math Wall," is designed to build mathematical understanding and procedural fluency. Students will visually display their problem-solving strategies and solutions, creating a gallery of worked examples for review and discussion. A monstrous visual example of math posted all around the room and another example of a visual study guide for students to build and see every day they walk into the classroom.

Materials:
- Poster paper or large sheets of butcher paper for displaying problems and solutions.
- Markers or pens for writing.
- Tape or magnets for affixing posters to the wall.
- Pre-selected math problems of appropriate difficulty for the class.

Activity Overview:
The "3D Math Wall" is an interactive activity where students work in groups to solve math problems. Each group is responsible for a different problem or set of problems. They will demonstrate their solutions on poster paper, which then becomes part of a classroom gallery of math strategies. This can be a non-competitive exercise or a timed challenge for an added element of fun and urgency.

Setup Instructions:
1. Assign each student group a section of wall space.
2. Post one or more math problems on each group's section of the wall.
3. Provide groups with poster or computer paper and markers to work out and display their solutions. Solutions running down or across the wall in large, neat, and organized print so they are easily seen and read from anywhere in the room.

Rules of the Activity:
1. Each group works together to solve the posted math problem(s) and demonstrates the solution process on their poster paper.
2. All steps must be shown clearly, with explanations as necessary to illustrate understanding.

3. After a set time, or once all groups have finished, the class can walk around to view each group's work and discuss different approaches.

4. If making it competitive, the fastest group with a correct solution can earn points or a reward.

Activity Variations:

+ For differentiation, assign more complex problems to groups ready for a challenge and more basic problems to others.
+ Introduce mixed operations or word problems to provide variety.
+ Allow for peer teaching, where students from each group explain their methods to the class.

Things to Consider:

+ Encourage students to think critically about the most efficient and clear way to present their problem-solving process.
+ Incorporate a timer to challenge groups to work not only accurately but also efficiently.
+ Keep track of time and accuracy for each group if incorporating competitive elements.
+ Consider awarding points for clarity of explanation, not just speed, to emphasize the learning process.

Closure:

Bring the class together to discuss the various problem-solving strategies used. Reflect on the importance of showing work and the benefits of collaborative problem solving. Use the completed "3D Math Wall" as a study resource for upcoming assessments.

Assessment:

Evaluate each group on their ability to accurately solve the problems, the clarity of their solution process, and their teamwork. Individually, assess students' understanding of the math concepts through their contributions to the group's work.

Sample Lesson Activity: Grading Papers

Objective:
The "Grading Papers" activity turns the tables, allowing students to act as the teacher by grading a set of posted test or review questions. Students love a chance to correct and "grade" the teacher! Students will "grade" the teacher by identifying correct answers/responses and correcting errors, reinforcing their understanding of the material and their attention to detail. This exercise not only serves as a fun way to review but also develops critical thinking and analytical skills.

Materials:
+ Fake test or review sheets with pre-written questions and answers, mounted around the classroom.
+ Blank sheets of paper or an answer sheet for each student to record and correct errors.
+ Pencils, pens, or markers for "grading."

Activity Overview:
In "Grading Papers," students are given the task of grading pre-prepared test questions that have been posted around the classroom. The answers to these questions are a mix of correct and incorrect responses. Students will analyze each one and determine its accuracy, providing corrections where necessary. This activity can be a fun and engaging way to review content and process information more deeply.

Setup Instructions:
1. Prepare a set of test or review questions relevant to the material recently covered.

2. Provide correct answers to some and deliberately incorrect answers to others.

3. Post these questions and answers around the classroom walls.

Rules of the Activity:

1. Each student is given a blank sheet of paper to record the questions and their "grades."

2. Students move around the room, reading each posted question and deciding if the answer is correct.

3. If an answer is incorrect, students must write down the correction on their sheet.

4. Encourage students to explain why an answer is incorrect when they write down their corrections.

Activity Variations/ Modifications:

+ Offer hints or additional resources for difficult questions to facilitate learning.

+ Have students work in pairs or small groups to discuss and agree on the corrections.

+ Peer Review Switch: After grading the posted questions individually, students pair up and exchange their papers to do a peer review. Each student checks the other's corrections and discusses any discrepancies they find.

+ Group Consensus Challenge: Students form small groups and must come to a consensus on the corrections for each question. This encourages debate and justification of their answers.

+ Correction Gallery Walk: Once all corrections are made, students do a gallery walk to see all the questions and answers. They can discuss the corrections as a class and learn from the mistakes.

+ Create-a-Test: After the activity, students create their own test question or questions and correct answers, demonstrating their understanding of the content and the correction process.

Things to Consider:
+ Provide a mini lesson on common mistakes or tricky concepts before the activity starts.
+ Offer points for each correct identification and accurate correction of an error.
+ Have a small reward for the student or group with the most correct "grades."

Closure:
Wrap up the activity by reviewing the most commonly missed questions and discussing the corrections. Highlight the value of learning from mistakes and the importance of reviewing work for errors. Discuss the role of a teacher in grading and how attention to detail can improve learning outcomes.

Assessment:
Evaluate students on their ability to correctly identify errors and make accurate corrections. Consider their explanations for why answers are incorrect to assess their depth of understanding. Assess their ability to work systematically and their engagement with the review process.

Sample Lesson Activity: Create-a-Test!

Objective:
In the "Create-a-Test" activity, students will apply their knowledge by formulating their own test questions and corresponding answers on recently learned material or as part of a review process. This exercise will assess students' grasp of the content and their ability to engage in the correction process critically. This simple to generate activity can be used in any grade level or content area and easily modified for varying degrees of difficulty based on the number of questions for students to generate, level of questions developed, and critical thinking involved.

Materials:
+ Notebooks or study materials for reference.
+ Paper and pens for writing questions and answers.
+ Access to research tools such as textbooks, library resources, or approved internet sites.

Activity Overview:
"Create-a-Test" challenges students to step into the role of the teacher by creating test questions with an answer key that demonstrates their content understanding. This task not only verifies their grasp of the material but also encourages higher order thinking as they develop questions that require critical thinking and deep comprehension.

Setup Instructions:
1. Review the content that students should focus on for their test questions.
2. Provide guidelines on the types of questions they can create (multiple choice, short answer, essay, etc.).
3. Explain how to formulate an 'answer key' with correct answers and justification.
4. Students can work individually or in student groups.

Rules of the Activity:
1. Each student group or individual student develops one or more test questions related to the content area.
2. Students write out the correct answer(s) for each question, explaining the rationale behind the answer on a separate answer key.
3. Encourage the creation of various question types to challenge different aspects of content mastery.

Activity Variations:

- Partner Work: Students can pair up to create a test together, promoting collaboration.
- Group Challenge: Groups of students create a full test, with each member responsible for a section.
- Peer Swap: After creating their tests, students swap with a classmate to answer each other's questions.

Things to Consider:

- Provide a short mini lesson on writing good test questions and what makes an answer comprehensive and complete.
- Review the student-created questions and answers, providing feedback on the quality and accuracy.
- Optionally, hold a vote for the most creative or challenging test question.
- Have student groups where students are tasked with answering a sample of questions from one another.
- To enhance student engagement and activity buy-in, consider telling students you will take a couple of most well written and thought out questions to add to a quiz or test.

Closure:

Conclude the activity with a class discussion about the experience of creating test questions and the insights gained into the learning and assessment process. Highlight the importance of understanding both sides of a test—the questioning and the answering.

Assessment:

Evaluate students on the clarity, relevance, and rigor of their test questions, as well as the accuracy and thoroughness of their answer keys. Consider their ability to use resources effectively and their engagement with the content through the question-creation process.

Sample Lesson Activity: Quick Hands!

Objective:

"Quick Hands!" is a dynamic and competitive classroom activity designed to engage students actively in reviewing and reinforcing content knowledge. Whether revisiting old material or reinforcing new concepts, using a competitive element to energize the learning process.

Materials:

- A marker or any small object that can be easily grabbed.
- Desks or tables arranged for one-on-one or group competition.
- Study materials and resources or notebooks to reference.

Activity Overview:

In "Quick Hands," students face off in pairs or teams with a simple objective: be the first to grab the marker after a question is asked and then correctly answer the question to earn a point. This activity not only encourages students to be attentive but also to be quick in recalling information from various resources or to study old content the night before, providing a lively way to review material. Be sure to provide a few seconds for students to think through the question before you prompt them to grab the marker or object in order to answer aloud.

Setup Instructions:

1. Arrange the classroom so that desks are in pairs or small circles for group competitions.
2. Place a marker in the center of each student pair or table for group setup.
3. Prepare a list of questions related to the content being reviewed.

Rules of the Activity:

1. Two students stand or sit at each desk, facing each other with the marker in between them.

2. The teacher asks a question related to the course content.

3. After a brief pause to think, the teacher says, "Go!" The first student to safely grab the marker can answer.

4. If the answer is correct, the student earns a point. If not, the opportunity to answer passes to the other student.

5. Students rotate after each question to ensure everyone gets a chance to participate.

Activity Variations:

- Team Play: Groups of four or five compete, with one representative from each group participating per round.

- Multiple Simultaneous Matches: Several pairs or groups answer questions at the same time around the classroom, increasing the energy and dynamic of the activity.

- Championship Round: The students or teams with the highest points face off in a final round to declare the ultimate champion.

- A math variation could be an equation is posted and students get 2 minutes to work out each problem then face off in a round of "Quick Hands" for the opportunity to share their mathematical solutions to earn points for their groups.

Things to Consider:

- Encourage students to use their study materials to review while waiting for their turn, reinforcing good study habits and the use of class resources.

- Implement time limits on how long a student can take to answer after grabbing the marker to maintain a brisk pace.

- Questions, content, and the time permitted can all be modified to fit the needs of your grade level, content, and student groups.

Scoring and Competition:

- Track points for each correct answer individually or by team.
- Consider offering small incentives or privileges for winning individuals or teams to motivate competitive spirit. For example, a homework credit, extra points on a quiz or assignment, or rewarding the whole class for a great effort by taking away or eliminating an extra class/homework assignment. This will also increase buy-in with future similar activities.

Closure:

Wrap up the session with a review of the questions asked and the correct answers, discussing any common errors or misunderstandings. Highlight effective strategies for quick recall and the benefits of having a good notebook, folder, or proper resources and active learning.

Assessment:

Assess students based on their participation and accuracy of answers. Consider their ability to use resources effectively and how actively they engage with the material both during and in preparation for the activity.

Sample Lesson Activity: Headbands Vocabulary Review

Objective:

"Headbands Vocabulary Review" is a dynamic classroom activity modeled after the fun party game/app. This activity is designed to reinforce vocabulary knowledge through active participation and recall. This game focuses on reviewing important terms, people, events, or phrases relevant to the subject matter, encouraging students to use clues, definitions, and synonyms to guide the teacher to the correct term on a notecard.

Materials:
- Notecards with vocabulary words, names, or phrases written on one side.
- Timer (I just use my timer on my iPhone) for tracking time during the activity.
- Optional: Whiteboard or Score Board on paper to put up on your wall or board to track best class times or group scores.

Activity Overview:

In this engaging and fast-paced review game, the teacher uses a stack of notecards, each bearing a term to be reviewed. One at a time, the teacher shows the notecard to the class without looking at the word, and students provide clues without saying the actual word. The teacher guesses the term based on student clues, which can include definitions, related events, synonyms, or other creative prompts. This is a timed activity so the best group or class time wins.

Setup Instructions:
1. Prepare a stack of notecards with terms from recent lessons.
2. Arrange the classroom so all students can see the teacher during the game.
3. Explain the rules and the objective of providing clues to guess the vocabulary term, phrase, event, or important name or concept.
4. Students may have notebooks and study materials and resources out to be ready for the most difficult notecards. This is a great way to reinforce using materials and studying.
5. Consider making review sheets or study guides with a list of the notecard terms for students to make individually to practice at home or with partners at the end of class to prepare.

Rules of the Activity:

1. This is best when it is a multi-day/round activity that is timed. Best group or class time over a few days' wins.
2. The teacher holds up a notecard facing the students and tries to guess the word based on student definitions, clue prompts, and synonyms.
3. Students cannot use part of the word in their clues but should use definitions, synonyms, or related facts and information. Rewording definitions and information are great ways to assess student content retention.
4. The activity is timed, and the goal is to get through as many cards as possible in the shortest amount of time.

Activity Variations:

- Allow students to form small groups and take turns being the guesser while others provide clues.
- Incorporate a "lightning round" where clues must be given in quick succession.
- Use a theme for each round, focusing on specific types of vocabulary such as only people, events, or critical terms.

Things to Consider:

- Start with a smaller set of notecards and gradually increase the number as students become more comfortable with the game.
- Challenge students to improve their time with each round, fostering a competitive and fun environment.
- Students who struggle with quick answers and need time to answer – prompt those students to be ready for a specific notecard or two and each round try to add another, so they slowly build their content retention.
- For students who overtake the crowd because they know all the answers fastest, tell them they are only allowed to answer 3 or

5 so pick the toughest cards to best help their classmates win in the end. This is a way to make sure students don't overtake the activity and all have a chance to participate.

+ For very young students this game could be modified for letter sound recognition or sounding out words and in this case call out the word on the notecard.

Scoring and Competition:

+ Keep track of the time it takes for the class to get through the stack of cards.
+ Post the best times on the classroom wall as a motivating leaderboard.
+ Reward the class or group that achieves the best time over a set period, like a week or unit.

Closure:

Discuss strategies that were effective and explore why certain words were more challenging than others. Allow students to reflect on their learning and how this activity might help them on upcoming tests or assessments.

Assessment:

Assess students based on their participation and the appropriateness and creativity of their clues. Evaluate their understanding of the vocabulary based on the accuracy of the clues they provide and their engagement in the game. Consider their teamwork and communication skills, especially in group settings.

Sample Lesson Activity: Bluffing

Objective:

"Bluffing" is an effective and energetic strategy game designed to review and reinforce new and old content knowledge across any grade level and subject. This activity encourages students to participate actively, whether they know the answer or not, and challenges them to strategically decide when to take risks. It also offers a fun, competitive way to engage all students in learning and recall.

Materials:
- Paper or small whiteboards and markers for each student to write down answers.
- Dice or a digital number scrambler for selecting student numbers who will show their answers to earn groups for their team.
- A scoreboard to keep track of team points.

Activity Overview:
In the game of "Bluffing," students are divided into teams and provided with markers and paper/ mini whiteboards to write their answers to questions posed by the teacher. Each student in the group will be given a number to either write on their desks or answer sheets. For example, in groups of 6 all groups will have a student number from 1-6. The teacher will first post the question or verbally ask a content related question and provide students with think time and time to write their answers down. Each student who knows the answer will stand. Students can choose to stand if they believe they know the answer, earning points for their team, or "bluff" and stand even if uncertain. The teacher will roll dice or use a number generator to randomly select students to show their answers, adding an element of chance to the strategy of standing or sitting.

Setup Instructions:
1. Divide the class into teams (consider gender, random groups, split-class groups, or other criteria).
2. Assign each team member a number, which they write on their desk or paper.

3. Prepare a list of questions relevant to the current topic of study.

Rules of the Activity:
1. The teacher asks a question related to the lesson or review material.
2. Students write their answers on paper within a certain time limit (30 seconds to 1 minute) and decide whether to stand (indicating confidence or bluffing).
3. Each standing student potentially earns one point for their team.
4. Using a dice or number scrambler, the teacher randomly selects students to reveal their answers. For example, dice lands on 5– all students who are number 5 turn your answer around for us to see.
5. Correct answers confirm the point; incorrect answers may lead to no points or a penalty, depending on teacher preference. If a student doesn't know the answer but was bluffing and stood but their number wasn't called to show their answer they could potentially earn a point for their team if not called on to answer.

Activity Variations:
+ Introduce "double or nothing" rounds where students can earn double points for correct answers or lose points if wrong.
+ Allow teams to challenge another team's answer to earn extra points. This is a great enhancement tool for later rounds to build excitement. For example a group can call out a number they wish to challenge and that student number in all groups have to turn their answer sheets around so all students can see what their answer was.
+ Use different types of questions (multiple choice, true/false, short answer) to vary the challenge and difficulty depending on your grade and student academic levels.

Things to Consider:

+ Encourage students to use their notes and textbooks to come up with answers, reinforcing good study habits.
+ Set a timer for answering and deciding to stand to maintain a brisk game pace to allow for more content to be covered during a class period.

Scoring and Competition:

+ Track points on a scoreboard visible to all students.
+ Celebrate the team with the highest score at the end of the game or class period.

Closure:

Discuss strategies that led to correct or incorrect answers and the risks and rewards of bluffing. Reflect on what students learned about the topic and about their own and their peers' thought processes. Go over the more difficult questions at the end.

Assessment:

Evaluate students on their participation and willingness to engage with the material, regardless of their confidence in each answer. Assess how well they understand the content based on the accuracy of their answers when called upon. Consider their strategic thinking in choosing when to bluff and when to rely on their knowledge.

Sample Lesson Activity: The Great Literacy Race

Objective:

"The Great Literacy Race" is a gamified group activity centered around literacy and designed to enhance reading comprehension and critical thinking. This strategy is a great way to turn a worksheet into a cooperative interactive activity. Students work collaboratively to identify key information from a text, discuss their findings, and quickly retrieve details to answer questions. This competitive reading game encourages meticulous reading, attention to detail/ note taking, and teamwork. This activity, however, could be modified and differentiated to be used in a group math challenge with similar question and answer options.

Materials:

- ✦ Copies of the same text document for each student.
- ✦ Highlighters and pens for marking important text features.
- ✦ A smart board or another method to display questions.
- ✦ Expo markers or paper for writing answers.
- ✦ A scoreboard for tracking points.

Activity Overview:

In "The Great Literacy Race," students are divided into small collaborative groups and given a text to read and analyze. After a designated reading period (ex. 10 minutes), they get set time (ex. 5 minutes) to go around one by one sharing insights with their group while group mates add those notes before entering a fast-paced question-and-answer game that tests their ability to find and articulate information from the text quickly. So it is imperative that students take their time reading through and critically analyze and think through the important aspects of the text document.

Setup Instructions:

1. Divide students into groups, providing each group with copies of the same text.
2. Distribute highlighters and pens for students to use during their reading.
3. Set up a smart board or prepare to read questions aloud for the race.

Rules of the Game:

1. Allow students ten minutes to read the text, during which they should highlight, underline, and make notes on important information in the margin.
2. After reading, give groups five minutes to discuss and share their findings, ensuring all members note the important points.
3. Post a question related to the text on the smart board or read it aloud. Students race to find the answer in the text and write it down using the expo marker or on group paper.
4. Once an answer is written, all group members must raise BOTH of their hands as if they were on a roller coaster to signal, they are done!
5. The teacher rushes over to quickly check answers: the first group with a correct answer earns 2 points, while other groups correctly answering within 20 seconds earn 1 point. Modify times based on student groups and age.

Activity Variations:

+ Introduce bonus rounds where answers can earn double points.
+ Use different types of texts (narrative, expository, historical) to vary the difficulty and skills practiced.
+ Allow groups to challenge another group's answer to earn extra points.

Things to Consider:

+ Encourage students to use skimming and scanning techniques to find answers quickly.
+ Challenge groups to improve their response times with each round to foster a sense of urgency and competition.
+ Provide struggling readers with the text ahead of time or the night before to give them an opportunity to get comfortable with the reading.

+ Modify rules for content like math or age, grade, academic and reading levels.

Scoring and Competition:

+ Keep a tally of each group's points on the scoreboard.
+ Celebrate the group with the highest score or groups that worked the hardest or had the best attitude during the activity regardless of score at the end of the game.

Closure:

Review the key points discussed during the activity and how they relate to the text's overall theme or subject. Discuss strategies that were effective and explore how this activity has helped enhance their reading comprehension skills.

Assessment:

Evaluate students based on their engagement in the activity, the accuracy of their responses, and their ability to work collaboratively in a group. Assess their notetaking and text analysis skills as well as their ability to recall information accurately.

Sample Lesson Activity: 4-Corners Review

Objective:

"4-Corners Review" is an engaging and interactive activity designed to review and reinforce content across any subject area. This game encourages students to think critically about multiple-choice questions and to justify their answer choices, enhancing their understanding and reasoning skills. This is a great way to turn a worksheet into an activity.

Materials:

- Poster papers with numbers 1 through 4, posted in each corner of the classroom to showcase in an obvious way the location choices for the activity.
- Smart board or another display for presenting questions.
- Various assignments (e.g., guided math questions, text analysis questions, or general review materials).

Activity Overview:

In "4-Corners Review," students actively participate in content review by choosing answers to multiple-choice questions and physically moving to the corner of the room associated with their selected answer. This method not only allows students to express their understanding but also to engage in peer discussion and higher order thinking in the defense of their choices.

Setup Instructions:

1. Number each corner of the classroom from 1 to 4 and post the numbers on large posters.
2. Prepare a series of multiple-choice questions related to the current unit of study, with each question having four possible answers.
3. Arrange a central starting point for students within the classroom.

Rules of the Activity:

1. Display a question with four possible answers on the smart board.
2. Students decide on their answer choice and move to the corresponding numbered corner.
3. Once all students are in their corners, select random students to explain why they chose their specific answer.

4. Reveal the correct answer and discuss why it is correct, addressing misconceptions if necessary.
5. Continue with additional questions, allowing students to move to the corner that represents their new answer choice each time.

Activity Variations:
+ Introduce a point system where students earn points for correct answers and additional points for successfully defending their choice.
+ Implement time limits for answering and moving to corners to add urgency and excitement.
+ Organize students into small groups or peer grouping instead of individuals, promoting teamwork and collaborative decision-making.

Things to Consider:
+ Encourage students to use critical thinking and justification skills to defend their answers with evidence depending on the resources provided.
+ Keep a tally of points for correct answers and successful defenses per individual or student group.
+ Consider ending class with an individual "quick-set" of questions asked during the activity to assess student learning and understanding.
+ Consider offering a small reward or privilege to the group or individual with the highest score at the end of the game or provide the whole class with a reward for having fun while activity participating in the learning activity. This will reinforce effort, positive student interactions, and active learning.

Closure:
Conclude the activity with a class discussion on the strategies used to choose and defend answers. Reflect on the learning process and the

effectiveness of moving and discussing in helping to solidify understanding of the content.

Assessment:
Evaluate students based on their participation in the activity, the accuracy of their answers, and their ability to articulate and defend their choices. Assess their engagement with the content and their ability to apply critical thinking and reasoning during the review.

Sample Lesson Activity: Is it TRUE?

Objective:
"Is it TRUE?" is an activity designed to enhance critical thinking and content review by challenging students to discern the truth among multiple similar options. Modeled after the concept of identifying reality versus imitation in the Netflix Original Gameshow "Is It CAKE?" This activity encourages students to apply their knowledge to determine which of the three presented questions or statements is a decoy and which is correct.

Materials:
+ Smart board or other display to post questions or statements.
+ Small white boards or paper for groups to record their answers in real time.
+ Optional: game show music to play during decision-making time to give the activity more of an authentic gameshow feel.

Activity Overview:
In "Is it TRUE?" students work in groups to identify the correct question or statement among three options, two of which are cleverly crafted decoys. This game is structured in rounds, with each round

increasing in point value, creating a fun and competitive atmosphere that encourages engagement and application of lesson content. Point values and the number of rounds/questions are up to the teacher based on difficulty needs and modifications for student learning.

Setup Instructions:
1. Prepare three similar question/answers or fact statements per round, ensuring that only one is correct. Depending on student levels make decoy answers or statements very close to the correct answer. Math Ex. $3x+5=20$ $x=5$ or decoy ($3x+5=20$ $x=4$)
2. Display the three options on the smart board for all students to see.
3. Arrange students into small groups, providing them with small smart boards or paper to record their answers.

Rules of the Activity:
1. Display the three questions or statements related to the current study topic.
2. Give groups a set amount of time to discuss and decide which one is the true or correct answer.
3. Play fun, motivating music during the "student work time" to enhance the game-like atmosphere.
4. At the end of the time, groups write down their choice on their smart board or paper.
5. Reveal the correct answer and award points to groups who chose correctly.
6. Increase the point value with each subsequent round for added excitement.

Activity Variations:
+   Include visual clues or additional hints that might help in solving more complex questions.

+ Implement bonus rounds where students can earn extra points for providing a justification for their choice.
+ Use multimedia elements to present the questions or statements, such as video clips or animations, especially for topics like history or science.
+ Add extra point or points for the first group to choose the correct answer and verify with the teacher.

Things to Consider:
+ Encourage students to use deduction skills and available resources to differentiate between the nearly identical options.
+ Set time limits for each round to maintain a brisk pace and keep students focused.
+ Allow students to use resources to reinforce the use of notes, maps, literacy assignments previously used in class.

Scoring and Competition:
+ Keep a running tally of each group's points, displayed publicly to foster a competitive spirit.
+ Consider rewarding the winning group with a class privilege or small prize at the end of the game.

Closure:
Discuss the strategies that successful groups used to identify the correct answers. Reflect on how this activity helps in understanding key concepts and improving analytical skills. Explore the importance of attention to detail and critical evaluation in learning.

Assessment:
Evaluate students based on their engagement in the activity, the accuracy of their answers, and their ability to collaborate effectively with

peers. Assess how well students can justify their choices and use logical reasoning to approach the challenges.

Sample Lesson Activity: Boom, Clap, Grab

Objective:

"Boom, Clap, Grab" transforms traditional worksheet tasks into a lively gamified group activity that combines physical movement with academic review. This game is designed to engage students in active review of any content, making learning interactive and fun. It encourages quick individual thinking and teamwork depending on how you set up the activity, while reinforcing content comprehension.

Materials:

- Text documents or worksheets for initial review.
- Notecards, one per group, folded and inverted for easy grabbing.
- A space in the classroom where groups can sit in circles.

Activity Overview:

In "Boom, Clap, Grab," students start by reviewing a text document or completing guided math problems to refresh their knowledge. They then form small groups, each with a notecard placed in the center. The teacher integrates physical actions (Boom and Clap) with the challenge of grabbing the notecard on the cue of "GRAB," followed by a rapid question-and-answer session. This game not only reviews academic content but also adds a kinetic element to learning.

Setup Instructions:

1. Distribute the text documents or worksheets for students to analyze and note important information or allow students to work through review math problems or content questioning from provided resources.

2. Arrange students into small groups of 2-5 and have them stand in circles around a table or desks pushed together. Allowing each student with the ability to grab the inverted notecard.
3. Place one folded, inverted notecard in the center of each group.

Rules of the Activity:
1. Students begin by reviewing their documents, highlighting key information or solving content problems.
2. The teacher starts the gamified activity by giving verbal cues: saying "Boom" means students pat their thighs, and "Clap" means they clap their hands. These cues are given in a random sequence. (ex. Boom, boom, clap, boom, clap …)
3. When the teacher shouts "GRAB," students quickly try to grab the notecard from the center.
4. After grabbing, students wait for the teacher's "GO" to start discussing and answering the question related to their initial review.
5. Students record points for correct answers or quickly write their answer or circle an answer choice provided on a teacher given resource.
6. Points are awarded as follows: 2 points to the student who grabs the notecard first and answers the question correctly, and 1 point to any student who answers the question correctly.

Activity Variations:
- Introduce more complex sequences of "Boom" and "Clap" to increase difficulty and engagement.
- Include bonus rounds where grabbing the card can earn extra points or provide advantages in the next round.
- Rotate roles within groups so different students have the chance to be the first to grab the card.

+ This strategy can also be modified into a community-building and relationship-building strategy rather than a content review activity.

Things to Consider:

+ Encourage students to apply critical thinking and recall skills quickly after the grab.
+ Use this strategy to get students laughing and having fun while discussing and reinforcing the importance of positive behavior interactions.
+ End class with a quick-check individual question and answer assessment based on the information and questions used during the activity. This also reinforces student active listening and participation. Even if they don't get the answer correct during the game they can get the question correct on the "quick-check" at the end of class.

Scoring and Competition:

+ Keep a running tally of points for each group or individual, displayed on the board for everyone to see or depending on student ages, have students keep a running tally. Students do a great job of making sure that other students are being honest in their responses.
+ Consider creating a playful competition atmosphere by having small prizes for the winning team or individual.

Closure:

Conclude the activity by discussing what strategies worked best for remembering and retrieving information. Reflect on the integration of physical activity and learning, and how it affected students' engagement and retention of content.

Assessment:
Evaluate students based on their active participation, ability to recall and apply content accurately, and teamwork during the game. Assess how well they were able to engage with the provided material and their effectiveness in communicating their answers during the game. You can also assess student content retention during a "quick-check" of individual questions like a mini-quiz at the end of the activity to reinforce active participation and listening.

Sample Lesson Activity: Pop It

Objective:
"Pop It" is a lively classroom activity designed to make reading and content review more engaging through cooperative learning and a bit of playful competition. This activity integrates text analysis, new content assessment, or math review with a game-like element involving balloons containing points, which adds an element of surprise and fun to the learning process.

Materials:
- Balloons, each with a small piece of paper inside indicating point variations (add points, lose points, swap points).
- Texts for analysis or worksheets with math problems or review questions.
- Whatever resources or materials needed to assess your student content understanding.
- Dice for selecting groups to pop balloons.
- Tape to attach balloons around the room.

Activity Overview:
In "Pop It," students work in small groups to analyze texts or content resources, answer review questions, or solve math problems, discussing

key concepts and answer choices. Following this review session, the teacher poses questions related to the content. Correct answers allow groups a chance to pop a balloon and reveal additional point opportunities, leading to an exciting review session that reinforces key learning objectives.

Setup Instructions:
1. Arrange students into cooperative peer groups and assign each a unique number. Ex. Groups 1-12
2. Prepare blown up balloons with points or special actions written on papers inside them, and tape these around the classroom.
3. Provide students with reading materials or assignments that need to be reviewed.

Rules of the Activity:
1. Groups spend initial time working through their assigned readings or problems, discussing, and analyzing the content.
2. The teacher asks a question related to the review material. Students are allowed to use materials and dive back into the resources provided to find the answer.
3. Groups can write down their answers or answer verbally.
4. If a group answers correctly, they are awarded base points (e.g., 1-5 points).
5. Next, the teacher rolls dice to select a group number or a series of groups. The chosen group then picks a balloon to pop with their pencil, revealing additional points or special actions like swapping points with another group.
6. Continue through multiple rounds, posing different questions and allowing groups multiple opportunities to earn points.

Activity Variations:
+ Include "challenge" balloons that offer double points or allow a group to answer an extra question for bonus points.

+ Include "actions" in the balloons like jumping jacks, jumping on one leg, or doing a funny dance for 5 seconds.

Things to Consider:
+ Encourage critical thinking and discussion within groups to solve problems or analyze texts effectively.
+ Introduce a time limit for discussions and answer phases to maintain a dynamic pace.

Scoring and Competition:
+ Track each group's points on a scoreboard, updating totals after each round.
+ Celebrate the group with the highest total points at the end of the game, while emphasizing the importance of participation and teamwork.

Closure:
Review the correct answers and discuss the best strategies used by groups. Highlight effective teamwork and praise students for their cooperative efforts. Reiterate the importance of enjoying the learning process and striving for personal and collective improvement, not just focusing on scores.

Assessment:
Evaluate students based on their participation in discussions, the accuracy of their answers, and their ability to work collaboratively in groups. Consider how well they apply critical thinking to analyze texts or solve problems and their
engagement in the competitive aspects of the game.

Sample Lesson Activity: 100's Chart Race

Objective:

The "100's Chart Race" is an engaging and energetic activity designed to transform traditional worksheet tasks into an interactive game. This activity facilitates review and reinforcement of content across any grade level and subject area, utilizing a 100's chart to visually track progress and encourage competition among groups. It is easily adaptable for different grade levels and subjects, promoting cooperative learning and strategic thinking.

Materials:

+ A 100's chart displayed on a smart board, or a large, laminated poster posted on your white board.
+ Dice to roll after each round.
+ A group marker with a picture taped or connected with a small magnet.
+ Review materials related to the lesson.

Activity Overview:

In the "100's Chart Race," students work in cooperative groups to answer questions related to a lesson taught using various resources. Each correct answer allows the group to roll a set of dice at a central desk next to the teacher at the front of the room so all students can see and hear what each group rolls—and advance on a 100's chart projected on the smart board. The goal is to see which group can move the furthest along the chart or reach 100 the fastest, turning routine review into an exciting race to the finish line.

Setup Instructions:

1. Teach a lesson using diverse resources such as literacy texts, math concepts, or other subject matter for any topic of choice.

2. Display a 100's chart on the smart board or as a large poster visible to all students.

3. Organize students into small cooperative learning groups.

Rules of the Game:

1. Following the lesson, pose a series of questions to the groups to assess content retention, related to the content discussed.

2. When a group answers a question correctly, they select one member to roll the set of dice at the front of the room where the teacher is located. One-by-one, quickly, each group rolls the dice.

3. The number on the dice determines how many spaces the group's marker located on the 100's chart with a magnet or tape moves forward on the 100's chart.

4. Continue asking questions, allowing groups to answer and roll the dice to progress on the chart.

Activity Variations:

+ Introduce challenge spaces on the chart where groups can earn double moves or answer bonus questions for extra points.

+ Include setback spaces where groups might roll back a few spaces to add an element of surprise and strategy.

+ Use different colored markers or logos to represent each group on the 100's chart.

Things to Consider:

+ Encourage quick and accurate responses to questions to keep the game pace lively.

+ Set a time limit for each question to heighten the urgency and challenge students to think and respond swiftly.

Scoring and Competition:
+ Track each group's progress on the 100's chart as they answer questions and roll the dice.
+ The first group to reach 100, or the group furthest along when time expires, wins the race.

Closure:
Conclude the activity with a discussion on the strategies that led to successful answers and progress on the chart. Review any difficult questions and correct misunderstandings. Emphasize the fun aspects of learning through games and the importance of teamwork in achieving goals.

Assessment:
Evaluate students based on their participation and teamwork, the accuracy of their responses, and their ability to engage with and understand the content. Assess how effectively groups collaborate and make strategic decisions during the race.

Sample Lesson Activity: FAST CASH

Objective:
"FAST CASH" is an energizing and interactive activity designed to reinforce and review content across any subject area. This is a great strategy to enhance student engagement by gamifying review and turning a worksheet into an engaging learning experience for students. By integrating fake money rewards into the activity, this game enhances engagement and motivation among students, encouraging them to participate actively in answering questions to earn cash for their group. The goal is to accumulate the most "cash" by the end of the game.

Materials:
- Printed fake money in various denominations ($1, $5, $10, $20, $100).
- Envelope, bag, or hat to hold the fake money.
- A series of worksheets or questions based on recent lessons.
- A scoreboard or method to track each group's earnings.

Activity Overview:
In "FAST CASH," students work in groups to answer review questions from recent lessons. Each correct answer entitles the group to draw a bill from a collection of fake money, without looking, to add to their group's total. This adds an element of chance and excitement to the review process, as groups compete to see who can earn the most money before the final round and the activity ends!

Setup Instructions:
1. Prepare review materials and questions relevant to the content recently covered in class.
2. Print and cut out fake money in various denominations and place them in a container.
3. Organize students into cooperative groups.

Rules of the Activity:
1. Pose questions to the groups related to the lesson content.
2. Allow groups a few moments to discuss and provide an answer.
3. If a group answers a question correctly, they send one member to draw a bill from the money container.
4. The drawn bill's amount is added to the group's total cash.
5. Continue with more rounds of questions, allowing groups multiple chances to earn money.

Activity Variations:

+ Introduce "jackpot" questions that allow groups to draw two or more bills if answered correctly.

+ Include "tax" or "penalty" bills that might require groups to pay back or "lose" some of their earnings or even give a chance to steal from another group.

+ Offer bonus rounds where groups can bet some of their cash to double their earnings on particularly tough questions.

Things to Consider:

+ Encourage strategic thinking and teamwork, as groups decide who will answer and when to take risks on difficult questions.

+ Encourage students to use all resources from previous class activities. This is a great way to reinforce organization and use of information and study habits.

+ Implement timed rounds to keep the pace lively and prevent groups from taking too long to answer.

Scoring and Competition:

+ Keep a visible tally of each group's cash total to foster a competitive atmosphere.

+ The group with the highest amount of cash at the end of the game is declared the winner.

Closure:

Review the key points covered during the game and discuss the correct answers to the questions. Highlight effective strategies and decisions made by groups. Conclude by emphasizing the importance of teamwork and knowledge in winning the game and reflect on how this fun activity relates to managing real-world finances and decision-making.

Assessment:

Evaluate students based on their participation, the accuracy of their responses, and their ability to work effectively in groups. Assess how well they understand and retain the content, as well as their engagement and enthusiasm during the activity.

Sample Lesson Activity: Be the Teacher Podcast

Objective:

"Be The Teacher Podcast" is an innovative but simple to create activity where students take on the role of a teacher by creating their own educational podcast recording. This project allows students to research or create a verbal review of content, articulate their knowledge clearly, and engage in teaching, thus reinforcing their understanding. It's adaptable for any age, grade level, and subject area.

Materials:

- Recording devices (such as tablets or computers with microphones).
- Software or apps for recording and editing audio (if available).
- Materials for research and outline/scriptwriting (notebooks, textbooks, internet access for research).
- Guidelines for creating a podcast and a rubric for assessment.

Activity Overview:

Students work in collaborative groups to create a podcast episode. They start by researching and scripting a detailed outline that covers key topics and potential information the listener would need to answer test questions. The podcast is designed to teach future learners about a specific subject, culminating in the creation of a student generated written test to assess understanding of the discussed content (questions to go along with their podcast).

Setup Instructions:

1. Introduce the concept of a podcast and discuss guidelines to help students create their content.
2. Assign students into peer or small groups and assign them a specific content area to cover. For example, chapter 3 or section 1 of chapter 3 or a specific unit topic of study.
3. Provide resources and tools for research, scriptwriting, and recording.

Rules of the Activity:

1. Each group develops a descriptive outline that includes key topics and questions that someone would need to understand to pass a test on the subject.
2. Groups write a fluid script to work off for their podcast, ensuring it includes clear explanations and engaging elements to teach listeners what they need to know to pass the student created assessment or your unit test for that topic.
3. After scripting, groups record their podcast, practicing speaking clearly and engagingly.
4. As an additional component, each group creates a short assessment of a few questions to go along with their podcast content.

Activity Variations:

+ Groups could produce a series of shorter episodes covering different aspects of the topic rather than one long episode.
+ Introduce a peer review phase where groups exchange podcasts and provide feedback before final submission.
+ Depending on academic level or age, allow groups to use multimedia elements in their podcasts, such as sound effects or music, to enhance the listening experience.

Things to Consider:

+ Encourage critical thinking as students decide what information is essential for understanding the topic. "What do I need to know?"
+ Time management becomes a crucial skill as groups must plan, script, record, and edit their podcasts within a set timeframe.
+ Use a rubric to assess the podcasts based on content accuracy, clarity of explanation, creativity, and presentation.
+ Optionally, podcasts can be shared with the class or other audiences, and students can "peer-edit" offering suggestions or topics to add.

Closure:

Wrap up the project with a class listening session of the podcasts, followed by a discussion of what was learned from the experience. Discuss the different approaches groups took and the effectiveness of teaching through audio media.

Assessment:

Evaluate students based on their research, scriptwriting, final podcast, and written assessment. Assess how effectively they translated content knowledge into an educational format and their ability to work collaboratively on this project. Consider their use of technology and media to enhance educational delivery.

Sample Lesson Activity: Student-Teacher Videocast

Objective:

"Student-Teacher Videocast" is an immersive activity where students step into the role of an instructor by creating a video recording of a teaching session. This project is designed to deepen students' understanding and mastery of content by preparing and delivering a lesson as if students were in front of a classroom of students simulating a real classroom teaching experience. It can be adapted to any subject and grade level, enhancing both their knowledge and presentation skills.

Materials:
+ Video recording devices (laptops, tablets, or whatever school recording devices you have available).
+ Whiteboards or large sheets of white construction paper as makeshift whiteboards as if students were presenting in front of a classroom.
+ Markers for the whiteboards.
+ Tripods or stable desk/table setups to hold recording devices.
+ Resources for content research and lesson planning.

Activity Overview:
Students will work in collaborative peer groups to prepare and record a videocast where they teach a specific topic or unit of study as if they were in front of a classroom. This involves researching the topic, creating a detailed outline, scripting the lesson, and using a whiteboard to illustrate key points and concepts, just like a teacher would.

Setup Instructions:
1. Brief students on the fundamentals of creating educational videos, including aspects of engaging teaching and effective visual aids.
2. Assign topics or let students choose from a list of topics relevant to the current curriculum.
3. Provide time for students to research their topics, organize their lessons, practice the teaching component, and prepare any visual aids they will use on the whiteboard.
4. Set up areas with whiteboards or white construction paper where students can record their teaching sessions.

Rules of the Activity:

1. Each student or group creates a detailed lesson plan, which should include an introduction to what will be taught, main content delivery, and a conclusion that reinforces the key learnings. "Today you will learn how to solve..."
2. Students record their teaching session, ensuring they clearly explain the concepts and effectively use the whiteboard to illustrate their points and show examples or key notes.
3. Encourage students to practice their presentation skills, focusing on clarity of speech, engagement techniques, and professional demeanor.
4. After recording, students can edit their videos to enhance clarity and engagement, if necessary and if equipment and skills permit.

Activity Variations:

- Include peer reviews where students watch and provide constructive feedback on each other's videos before final submission.
- Challenge students to incorporate interactive elements, such as questions for the class, to make their videos more engaging.
- Allow advanced students to use video editing software to add additional educational graphics or effects. For example, windows media, iMovie, or another similar app. Students can even find their own and often find better technology options that would enhance the lesson.

Things to Consider:

- Enhance digital literacy and multimedia skills through the process of outline and lesson creation, filming, and editing.
- Encourage effective public speaking and presentation skills in a controlled setting.

Scoring:

+ Use a rubric to evaluate the videos based on content accuracy, presentation skills, creativity, and use of visual aids if needed.
+ Optionally, videos can be shared with the class or a wider audience, with awards for categories like "Best Teaching," or "Most Creative" for example.

Closure:

Conclude the activity by having a class viewing of the videocasts, followed by a reflective discussion on what was learned from the experience. Discuss the different teaching styles observed and the effectiveness of using visual aids. Consider discussing how difficult it is to teach and use this as an additional conversation around giving teachers grace and support. Now they understand a small portion of what we go through.

Assessment:

Evaluate students based on the depth and accuracy of their content, the clarity and engagement of their presentation, and their ability to utilize visual aids effectively. Assess how well they managed the project from planning through to the final product.

Sample Lesson Activity: Unit/Topic Sketch-Note

Objective:

"Unit/Topic Sketch-Note" is a simple to create activity that encourages students to synthesize key concepts visually and creatively from a chapter or unit into a comprehensive educational poster. This creative activity enhances understanding by requiring students to represent complex information through engaging images and concise written descriptions, centered around a clearly defined theme.

Materials:

- Poster paper.
- Markers, colored pencils, and crayons.
- Access to textbook or additional materials such as computers or tablets for image research (optional).
- Printers for printing images (optional).
- Scissors and glue for creative added elements (pop-up pictures or printed images etc.)

Activity Overview:

Students will create a sketch-note that visually maps out a chapter or unit of study teaching main ideas and key information. This sketch-note will act as a visual and descriptive topic study guide for an assessment. The main title or theme will be prominently displayed in the center of the poster, with related images and short descriptions branching out as mini-themes. This layout helps depict the connections among various concepts within the overall topic, making the sketch-note both an informative and visually appealing learning tool.

Setup Instructions:

1. Assign each student or group a specific chapter or unit from their textbooks. All students or groups typically would have the same topic.
2. Provide all necessary materials for creating the sketch-notes.
3. Introduce the sketch-note concept, emphasizing the importance of a central theme surrounded by related mini-themes.
4. Provide examples of high-quality sketch-notes as well as discuss successful approaches and problems that may occur in which to avoid.
5. Always set up a rough draft.

Rules of the Activity:

1. Students review their assigned content to identify the central theme, key concepts, and supporting details.
2. The central theme should be written prominently in the middle of the poster.
3. Students then create images and write descriptions for mini-themes that relate directly to the central theme, arranging these around the central title in a visually cohesive manner.
4. Images can be hand-drawn, traced off the computer, or printed. Tracing allows for poor illustrations to look perfect and for students to practice utilizing their resources and for unlimited creativity.
5. Descriptions should be concise and directly explain or complement the visuals.
6. The layout should enable a viewer to easily understand the flow of information and how each part relates to the central theme.

Activity Variations:

- Challenge students to be as creative as possible.
- Organize a "Sketch-Note Slam" where students present their posters to the class, explaining their design choices and the content covered.

Things to Consider:

- Foster students' abilities to analyze text and distill it into essential themes and ideas.
- Encourage artistic expression and precision in the way information is visually and descriptively communicated.
- Have peers and/or teachers rate each sketch-note based on creativity, accuracy, clarity of information, and aesthetic appeal.
- Offer recognition for categories such as "Most Creative Layout," "Best Use of Color," and "Most Informative."

Closure:

Wrap up the activity by having students reflect on their learning process and the effectiveness of using visual notes for study and revision. Discuss what worked well and what could be improved in future sketch-notes.

Assessment:

Assess students on the accuracy and description of the information presented, the clarity and relevance of the images and descriptions, and the overall organization and aesthetic of the sketch-note. Evaluate how well they connected the mini-themes to the central theme, demonstrating an understanding of the material's structure and content connections.

Sample Lesson Activity: Sketch-Noting Using AI Imaging

Objective:

Sketch-Noting using AI leverages modern technology to engage students in a unique and interactive way by utilizing AI-driven applications to create visual and descriptive study guides. This activity empowers students to explore how artificial intelligence can bring text-based content to life, providing an innovative approach to summarizing and presenting educational material. This is a very easy lesson idea to generate using free apps such as Canva's AI image generator and students will be super engaged creating real life images bringing content to life!

Materials:

+ Computers or tablets with internet access.
+ Access to AI-powered applications like Canva (free for teachers and students), which features an AI image generator.
+ Instructions and guidelines for activity and examples for using AI tools effectively. (Show students how easy and fun this is).

Activity Overview:
In the "Sketch-Note Using AI Imaging," students use AI tools to create a digital sketch-note that visually and descriptively using text represents a chapter, a book story, or any unit of study. By inputting short, detailed descriptions into an AI image generator, students can see how their written content is transformed into vivid, relevant images, enhancing their understanding and retention of the material and incorporating literacy. For young kids, provide sentence starters for them to type.

Setup Instructions:
1. Introduce students to the AI tools they will be using, such as Canva's AI image generator.
2. Provide a brief tutorial on how to use these tools to create digital sketch- notes. Students will want to spend hours creating examples so be prepared for students to be highly engaged with this.
3. Assign students specific topics or chapters for which they will create their sketch-notes.

Rules of the Activity:
1. Each student or group selects a topic or unit of study to work on.
2. Students research their chosen topic to gather comprehensive details and write concise descriptions that accurately convey the key concepts.
3. Using the AI image generator, students input their descriptions to create corresponding images.
4. Students compile these images along with additional textual explanations to form a coherent, descriptive, and visually engaging sketch-note.
5. Each sketch-note should be structured to accurately present information, with a clear flow that is easy to follow.

Activity Variations:

- Challenge students to use AI-generated images to explain complex concepts and add additional images to enhance the structure, testing the AI's ability to interpret and visualize academic content.
- Allow students to enhance their sketch-notes with multimedia elements such as videos or interactive links.
- Organize a showcase where students can present their AI-created sketch-notes to the class, explaining the process and their design choices.

Things to Consider:

- Encourage creativity and critical thinking as students decide how to best describe their topics for AI interpretation. Provide examples or descriptive sentence starters
- Teach students to critically evaluate the effectiveness and limitations of AI in educational content creation.

Scoring and Competition:

- Have a panel of judges (teachers or older students) assess the sketch-notes based on creativity, accuracy, and visual appeal.
- Provide feedback focusing on how effectively the AI images represented the content and the clarity of the accompanying descriptions.

Closure:

Conclude the activity with a discussion on the role of AI in education and its potential impact on learning and content creation. Have students reflect on their experiences with the AI tools and discuss the advantages and challenges they encountered. Have students discuss how AI helped them and increased their abilities and their attention to detail in their descriptions.

Assessment:

Evaluate students based on the detail of their content descriptions, the relevance and accuracy of the AI-generated images, and the overall aesthetic and descriptive clarity of the final sketch-note. Assess their ability to integrate technology with traditional educational methods and their adaptability in learning and applying new digital tools.

Sample Lesson Activity: Gallery Walk

Objective:

"Gallery Walk" is a simple to implement strategy that transforms a traditional worksheet into a classroom activity. This lesson engages students by allowing them to physically move around the room to answer questions posted on the walls, encouraging active learning, use of resources, and collaboration. It is ideal for reviewing material in any subject and can be adapted for varying levels of difficulty.

Materials:

+ Full sheets of computer paper for each question.
+ Tape or staples for posting questions on the walls.
+ Student notebooks or other resources for reference.
+ Timer for setting general time limits.

Activity Overview:

In the "Gallery Walk," questions from a typical worksheet are enlarged and posted around the classroom. Students are given a set amount of time to walk around and answer these questions, either individually or in small groups. This format not only helps to energize the learning environment by taking a sit-down worksheet and turning into a standup activity but also promotes independent and cooperative learning as students engage with the content at their own pace. Add point values to the questions to turn this activity into a classroom game or challenge.

Setup Instructions:

1. Select a worksheet that you plan to use for the lesson and enlarge each question onto a full sheet of computer paper.
2. Arrange the room by posting these questions on different walls or spaces around the classroom.
3. Organize students into individuals or teams, depending on your class dynamics and the objectives of the activity.

Rules of the Activity:

1. Provide each student or group with an answer paper to record their answers.
2. Set a timer for the duration of the activity to ensure that students use their time efficiently.
3. Students start the activity at a posted question of their choice and proceed to move through the questions at their own pace.
4. Encourage students to use their resources, such as notebooks or textbooks, to assist them in answering the questions. This is a great way to reinforce the importance of keeping a good notebook and keeping resources as well as good study habits.
5. After the timer ends, gather the students together to review the questions and discuss the answers as a whole group.

Activity Variations:

- Introduce bonus questions hidden around the room for additional points.
- Use different colored papers for different types of questions (e.g., blue for true/false, yellow for multiple choice).

Things to Consider:

- Develop students' time management skills by challenging them to answer all questions within the set time.

+ Enhance critical thinking and problem-solving as they apply learned material to answer questions making connections and showing understanding.

Scoring and Competition:
+ Allow students to just work on the questions or for added fun, assign points to each question, with students tallying their scores based on correct answers.
+ Consider offering a small reward or recognition for the highest scoring individual or team to add a competitive element.

Closure:
Wrap up the session by reviewing all the questions and correct answers, discussing common challenges or mistakes, and highlighting any interesting insights or alternative solutions provided by students. Provide feedback on the activity to gauge student content retention and understanding.

Assessment:
Evaluate students based on their participation and the accuracy of their answers. Consider their ability to work effectively in teams (if applicable) and their engagement with the activity. Assess how well they were able to apply classroom knowledge to solve the problems presented during the gallery walk by checking their answers or providing a post-activity assessment like an exit ticket.

Sample Lesson Activity: Movie Poster Advertisement

Objective:
"Movie Poster Advertisement" is a creative and engaging activity where students apply their understanding of a subject by designing a movie poster that effectively communicates a central theme. This project

encourages the integration of artistic design and literacy skills with educational content, using either digital tools like AI generators, Google Slides, PowerPoint, Canva, or traditional drawing methods.

Materials:

- Digital devices (computers, tablets) with access to design software or apps.
- Art supplies for hand-drawing (poster paper, markers, colored pencils, etc.).
- Examples of real movie posters for reference.
- Guidelines on poster design elements such as font styles, image placement, and information layout.

Activity Overview:

Students create a movie poster that advertises a fake "film" based on a topic they have studied. This involves designing a primary image that captures the essence of the theme, accompanied by supporting text elements such as a catchy title, a tagline, and informational text that aligns with typical but exciting movie poster designs.

Setup Instructions:

1. Begin with a discussion and analysis of various movie posters, focusing on design elements like font style, graphics, and the text placement of content information to explain the topic.
2. Assign students a specific theme related to the content they have been studying.
3. Provide access to the necessary digital tools or traditional art materials.

Rules of the Activity:

1. Students brainstorm and sketch preliminary designs for their movie posters creating an outline.

2. Have students get into peer groups with other groups (if they are already in a group) to discuss changes, aspects they like, and possible changes to make.

3. Using their chosen medium (digital or hand-drawn), students develop the main visual focal point for their posters. It is ok to allow students to trace–this is more about the idea not an art project. Allow students to use their resources here and trace all their cool ideas using their tablets or computers. Using AI image generators or other tech apps allows for unlimited creativity and options.

4. Add textual elements around the main image, including a title, a tagline or subtitle that captures the essence of the theme, and additional descriptive text.

5. Ensure that the design is cohesive and effectively communicates the assigned theme.

Examples for Implementation:

+   History Class: Students create a movie poster for a significant historical event, like the signing of the Declaration of Independence, featuring key figures as "stars" of the movie or other history events and people.

+   Science Class: Design a poster for a documentary-style movie about a major scientific elements, discovery, or theory, such as the planets or weather patterns or the water-cycle, using symbolic images and scientific facts to create something fun and exciting.

+   Literature Class: Students can design a poster for a film adaptation of a novel they have read, capturing the plot's essence or a critical character analysis in visual form.

Activity Variations:

+ Allow students to work individually or in small groups to foster collaboration or individual creativity.

+ Incorporate peer reviews where students give feedback on each other's designs before finalizing.

Things to Consider:

+ Enhance students' graphic design skills and their ability to convey information visually and textually.

+ Develop critical thinking by analyzing how best to represent complex themes in a visually appealing and informative poster.

+ Organize a gallery walk where students display their finished posters and vote on categories such as "Most Creative," "Best Design," and "Best Content Integration."

+ Use a rubric to assess each poster based on creativity, accuracy, and overall design.

Closure:

Conclude with a class discussion about the experience, what students learned about design and communication, and how visual elements can enhance the understanding of academic content. Review the design principles that were most effective across the projects.

Assessment:

Evaluate students on the clarity, creativity, and their ability to communicate and share "what I need to know about this topic" through text-features and the accuracy with which they represent the academic content, and the aesthetic quality of their designs. Consider their ability to synthesize information into a visually compelling advertisement.

Sample Lesson Activity: Creative Comic Strip

Objective:
"Creative Comic Strip" merges literacy, artistic expression, and digital skills into a dynamic assessment that gauge's students' understanding of specific content. This activity encourages students to synthesize information creatively and concisely, producing a 3-5 slide comic strip that narrates a topic through images and text to show understanding.

Materials:
- Art supplies such as paper, pencils, markers, and colored pencils for hand-drawn comics.
- Digital tools like tablets or computers with access to software and apps (Canva, Google Slides, PowerPoint, or AI image generators).
- Examples of comic strips for inspiration and structure understanding.

Activity Overview:
Students will create a short comic strip that visually and textually communicates a lesson or concept they have learned. They can choose to draw their comic strips by hand or utilize digital tools to create polished slides that combine images and text in a coherent narrative format.

Setup Instructions:
1. Introduce the project by showing examples of both traditional and digital comic strips. Discuss what to include and things to avoid or common mistakes.
2. Explain the comic strip requirements and the digital tools and materials available.
3. Assign or let students choose a content theme from recent lessons that they will convert into a comic strip narrative.

Rules of the Activity:

1. Students plan their comic strip, starting with a simple story-board that outlines the narrative across 3-5 slides.
2. Depending on their choice, students either draw their comic strips by hand or design them using the selected digital tools.
3. Each panel should include both images and text to effectively communicate the content theme. The text can include dialogue, captions, or thought bubbles.
4. Encourage the use of humor, drama, or action to make the comic engaging yet educational.

Activity Variations:

+ Allow students to work individually or in pairs to promote collaboration.
+ Have students incorporate specific artistic techniques or digital features that will help produce a better product.

Things to Consider:

+ Foster creativity in storytelling and visual representation.
+ Enhance digital literacy using various software and apps.
+ Develop planning and execution skills by managing the project from concept to completion within the set timeframe.

Scoring and Competition:

+ Organize a class exhibition of the completed comic strips and have students present their work to the class.
+ Use a rubric to evaluate the clarity of content communication, creativity, and overall presentation.
+ Consider peer voting for categories like "Most Creative," "Best Artwork," and "Best Content Explanation."

Closure:
Wrap up the project with a class discussion about the different creative approaches taken by students. Discuss the effectiveness of using visual narratives for learning and review key content points highlighted in the comic strips. Reflect on the skills learned during the project and how they can be applied to other subjects or projects.

Assessment:
Assess students on their ability to convey the assigned content theme clearly and creatively through their comic strips. Evaluate their use of text and imagery to create a coherent and engaging narrative showing and explaining "what I need to know" about the given topic and content. Also, consider their technical skills in using artistic or digital tools and their ability to work independently or collaboratively, depending on the project format.

Sample Lesson Activity: Grudge Ball

Objective:
"Grudge Ball" is an energetic classroom game that transforms traditional worksheets into a competitive and cooperative learning experience. This activity encourages students to engage deeply with content through guided math or reading, note-taking, and sharing before participating in a team-based game that involves strategy and physical activity.

Materials:
- Guided questions or text documents for initial student review.
- Whiteboard, smartboard, or large poster for tracking group scores.
- Markers to note group scores.
- Paper balls or soft foam balls.
- A trash can or designated basket.

Activity Overview:

In "Grudge Ball," students start by independently analyzing a text or solving math problems, noting key information. Groups then share their findings to ensure all members are prepared. The game portion involves answering questions to earn points or potentially remove points from other groups and shooting balls into a trash can to enhance their score manipulations. The objective is to maintain or regain their full points (X's) while attempting to reduce other groups' points.

Setup Instructions:

1. Divide students into cooperative learning groups.
2. Distribute the guided questions or text documents for students to review.
3. Set up the "Grudge Ball" scoreboard with each group's name and an initial number of X's (e.g., 5 X's per group).
4. Place the trash can at a reasonable distance for shooting the paper balls. As rounds continue make shots tougher but be conscious of student abilities. Making shots keeps them more engaged!

Rules of the Game:

1. Allow students time (e.g., 10 minutes) to read through the text or solve the problems, taking notes and highlighting important points.
2. Give groups an additional 5 minutes to share their notes or answers with each other, ensuring everyone is prepared.
3. Pose a question to the first group. If they answer correctly within 30 seconds or a given time, they choose another group to lose an X.
4. After answering correctly, a designated shooter from the group attempts to throw a paper ball into the trash can. Making the

shot allows them to remove an additional X from any group or to restore an X to their group (up to the starting maximum).

5. If a group answers incorrectly, the question passes to the next group.

6. Continue asking questions as groups try to stay in the game. You don't need a champion just to make students think there will be one group left – but you can play until certain groups are out of X's.

Game Variations:
+ Allow "knocked out" groups to earn re-entry into the game by assisting other groups or answering bonus questions.
+ Introduce special rounds where groups can earn double points or have a chance to revive all their X's.

Things to Consider:
+ Develop critical reading and problem-solving skills as students analyze texts or calculate answers.
+ Encourage teamwork and strategic thinking as groups decide whose X's to remove or restore. They MUST PICK DIFFER-ENT groups to spread out the elimination and make sure groups don't gang up on a certain team.

Scoring and Competition:
+ Track each group's remaining X's on the scoreboard.
+ The last group with X's remaining, or the group with the most X's at the end of the game, wins.

Closure:
Wrap up the activity with a discussion about the strategies used during the game and how the competitive element affected their engagement

and learning. Review the content covered in the questions to reinforce academic skills.

Assessment:

Evaluate students based on their ability to answer questions correctly, their engagement in the activity, and their teamwork. Assess how effectively they were able to communicate and collaborate during the note-sharing phase.

Sample Lesson Activity: Human BINGO

Objective:

"Human BINGO" transforms the traditional BINGO game into an active and engaging learning experience where students become "Human BINGO" pieces on a giant classroom BINGO board. This activity promotes teamwork, communication, and the application of knowledge as students collaborate to find answers to questions and achieve BINGO. Truly turning a worksheet into a fun and engaging learning experience!

Materials:
- Duct tape to create large BINGO cards on the classroom floor.
- Blown-up worksheet answers printed on large sheets of computer paper.
- Scissors to cut out the printed answers.
- Notebooks or other resources for students to reference.

Activity Overview:

In "Human BINGO," the classroom floor is turned into a large BINGO board with spaces big enough for students to stand in (ex. Each space is a floor tile). Create multiple taped BINGO cards spread throughout the classroom floor (2-3 total). Each group of students is given a set of large, printed answers that fit into the spaces on the BINGO board. One answer per space. The teacher reads clues or questions aloud, and students work together to find the correct answers, physically placing themselves and holding their answer sheets in the corresponding spots on the BINGO board.

Setup Instructions:
1. Use duct tape to mark out several large BINGO cards on the classroom floor, with each space big enough for a student to stand in.
2. Move desks and other furniture to clear space for the BINGO boards.
3. Print and cut out worksheet questions or answers to fit each box of the BINGO card, ensuring each group receives a complete set of answers.

Rules of the Game/Activity:
1. Divide students into groups, assigning each group to a BINGO card.
2. Distribute the cut-out answers to each group, with students placing one answer in each box on their group's BINGO card.
3. Students randomly spread the answer sheets into the box spaces on their team's Human BINGO card across the floor.
4. The teacher randomly selects and reads a question from the set.
5. Groups discuss and decide on the answer using their resources without sharing information with other groups.
6. A student from the group finds and picks up the corresponding answer sheet in the appropriate box on the BINGO card and stands in that space.
7. The first group to complete a line (horizontal, vertical, or diagonal) shouts "BINGO!" The teacher then verifies their answers.

8. The game can restart with new questions or continue to see how many BINGOs each group can achieve within a given time.

Game/Activity Variations:

- Include "challenge" questions that allow a group to place two answers at once if solved.
- Offer "bonus BINGO" rounds where certain lines or patterns score higher points.

Things to Consider:

- Encourage students to use critical thinking and problem-solving skills to quickly determine the correct answers.
- Develop teamwork and communication as students must work together efficiently under time constraints.

Scoring and Competition:

- Keep score of how many BINGOs each group achieves during the game with a scoreboard on your whiteboard or smartboard.
- Optionally, reward points for speed and accuracy, with additional points for completing more challenging BINGO patterns.

Closure:

Wrap up the session by discussing the activity's highlights and what strategies led to successful BINGO completion. Review the answers to ensure understanding of the material and reflect on how the game format affected students' engagement and learning.

Assessment:

Evaluate students based on their participation, the accuracy of their answers, and their ability to collaborate effectively. Assess how well they were able to integrate and apply their knowledge in a dynamic and competitive setting.

Sample Lesson Activity: The Bag Game

Objective:
"The Bag Game" transforms traditional worksheets into a fun, team-based activity that promotes engagement and collaboration. A simple strategy to turn review into an experience. This activity is designed to assess students' understanding of new topics or review materials such as guided math problems, text analysis, or other subject-specific questions in a fun and interactive format.

Materials:
+ Questions from a worksheet, each printed and cut out individually with a corresponding number.
+ Sandwich bags for holding the questions, one per group.
+ Tape or staples for attaching bags to a wall.
+ Markers for groups to write down their answers.
+ Desks or poster paper students will pre-number (Ex. from 1-10) for answer recording.

Activity Overview:
In "The Bag Game," each group receives a bag containing cut-out questions that they must answer within a set time. The game includes roles such as a runner, who retrieves questions from the bag but walks quickly and does not actually run, and researchers, who work together to find the correct answers. All students help with the research part. A writer/facilitator who writes the group answers in the correct spot depending on the question number. This setup encourages physical activity, teamwork, and effective use of learning resources.

Setup Instructions:

1. Prepare one worksheet per group by cutting out each question and placing them into a sandwich bag. Ensure each question is numbered.

2. Attach each bag to a wall on the opposite side of the classroom from where the corresponding group sits, using the group's number for identification.

3. Organize students into groups and assign roles: one runner, one writer/facilitator, and several researchers.

4. Arrange desks or set up poster paper where students will write their answers, ensuring each is numbered (Ex. from 1-10) in advance.

Rules of the Activity:

1. The game begins with the runner (walking quickly) fetching one question at a time from their group's bag. Runners cannot return to the bag until the answer is fully written down so the Runner must help with the research of an answer as well.

2. The group collaborates using their textbooks, notes, or other resources to find the answer.

3. The writer records the answer on the desk or poster paper under the corresponding question number.

4. Continue until all questions are answered or time runs out.

Activity Variations:

+ Play for fun, for % correct, or have a point scale with difficult questions being worth more points.

+ Introduce "challenge" questions that are worth more points if answered correctly.

+ Allow groups to use a "hint" card once or twice during the game, where they can ask for teacher assistance.

+ Implement bonus rounds where correct answers to difficult questions allow a group to take a second question during one run.

Things to Consider:
+ Foster quick decision-making and problem-solving as groups work under time constraints.
+ Enhance research skills and the ability to quickly locate information in text materials.

Scoring and Competition:
+ Award points for each correctly answered question.
+ Provide additional points for groups that complete all questions fastest or answer the most challenging questions correctly.

Closure:
Finish the activity with a group discussion to review all answers and clarify any misunderstandings. Highlight effective collaboration and communication within groups.

Assessment:
Assess their understanding of the material through the correctness of their answers and their ability to apply learning strategies effectively.

Sample Lesson Activity: Go Fish/Old Maid

Objective:
"Go Fish/Old Maid" takes the concept of classic card games and turns it into an educational matching game that reinforces vocabulary, review, and content understanding. In this activity, students play in pairs or small groups, using cards that feature questions on one card

and corresponding answers on another card. The objective is to match as many correct question-answer or vocabulary and definition pairs as possible.

Materials:

- Sets of note cards (one set per pair or group), each consisting of:
  - Card 1: Questions
  - Card 2: Corresponding Answers
- A container or envelope to hold the cards for each group. I typically end the previous class with students cutting out and gluing or writing on the cards to set them up for this activity. It gives them a sense of ownership over their cards.

Activity Overview:

Students will engage in a match-finding game where they work to pair questions with their correct answers. This activity is designed to promote critical thinking and memory recall of facts, and can be used to review vocabulary, historical facts, scientific concepts, math questions and answers, or any subject matter relevant to your curriculum. This is perfect for any age level.

Setup Instructions:

1. Prepare a set of cards for each group, with each card labeled clearly as either a question or an answer. Provide an answer key for each group to "double-check" answers for correct cards if needed.
2. Shuffle the cards well or have students shuffle cards and distribute them to each group, where students will spread all cards out on desks, floor, or tables face down from which players will flip over two at a time.
3. Explain the rules of the game, modeled after "Go Fish" or "Old Maid," adapted for educational content.

Rules of the Game/Activity:

1. Players will spread cards out on desks, floor, or tables face down flipping two cards at a time and try to match the question and answer or vocab and definition.

2. Players take turns flipping note cards finding the matching card to complete their question-answer pair. Turning over cards when they don't find the match. Checking the answer key if needed to be sure matching cards are correct.

3. If a player successfully matches a question with its answer, they place the pair down next to them and score a point. Trying to have the most pairs earning the most points for the round.

4. If no match is found, the player flips the card back over and the next player takes their turn.

5. The game continues until all cards have been matched or the allotted time ends. For example, each round is 7-10 mins.

Game/Activity Variations:

+ For larger groups, include multiple sets of the same question-answer pairs to make the game more challenging and competitive.

+ Adapt the game to different subjects by using different sets of question-answer pairs for topics like math problems and solutions, historical events and dates, or scientific terms and definitions.

Things to Consider:

+ Develop students' memory and recall abilities as they match questions and answers. This is an engaging way to review content.

+ Encourage cooperative learning and communication as students ask and answer questions within their groups.

Scoring and Competition:
- Award one point for each correctly matched pair.
- Keep track of each group's points and declare the group with the most matches the winner at the end of the game.

Closure:
Conclude the activity with a discussion about the questions and answers used in the game. Review any challenging pairs and clarify misunderstandings.

Assessment:
Evaluate students based on their participation, the accuracy of their matches, and their ability to collaborate and communicate effectively within their groups. Assess their recall of the subject matter and their strategic thinking during the game.

Sample Lesson Activity: SPLAT Review

Objective:
"SPLAT Review" is an energetic and interactive game that combines the use of pool noodles with academic review. Using foam pool noodles, students "splat" the correct answers to questions, making learning engaging and kinetic. This activity is perfect for reviewing any subject area and age level, encouraging quick thinking, and improving content recall.

Materials:
- Foam pool noodles, cut in half or thirds so they are more manageable.
- Paper with answers printed in large font, slightly larger than notecard size.
- Tape to secure answer papers on desks, floors, or tables.

+ A smart board or another method to display questions if needed (questions can also be called out verbally).

Activity Overview:
Students are divided into small groups, with answer sheets taped down within reach on desks or tables. Each round involves a question posed by the teacher, and students use pool noodles to physically "splat" the paper with the correct answer. Points are awarded for correct responses, with students rotating roles to keep the game engaging and inclusive.

Setup Instructions:
1. Prepare a set of printed answers and the teacher or students tape them down to the central locations of group desks or tables.
2. Distribute two or three pool noodles to each group.
3. Explain the game rules and discuss the importance of safety and fair play.

Rules of the Game/Activity:
1. Groups gather around their designated answer station with their pool noodles ready.
2. The teacher asks a question or displays it on the smart board.
3. The first student in each group to correctly "splat" the answer with their noodle scores a point for their group.
4. After each question, rotate the noodle to another group member to ensure everyone participates. Another option to play is winner stays in—this creates a fun and engaging competitive atmosphere depending on your group of students and their cooperative abilities.
5. Continue through a series of questions, tallying points for correct splats. Students can keep score or the teacher can create group score cards.

Game/Activity Variations:

- Introduce "double point" rounds for more challenging questions.
- Allow students to challenge a splat if they believe a wrong answer was hit, adding a review discussion to the game. Be sure to have students call out answers at the conclusion of the round to be sure students "splat" the correct answer choice.
- Include bonus rounds where students can earn extra points by answering additional questions without the noodle if they make a correct splat.

Things to Consider:

- Enhance students' quick thinking and reflexes as they must locate and splat the correct answer swiftly–but do not keep score and just have fun!

Scoring and Competition:

- Keep a visible tally of points for each group to foster a friendly competitive environment.
- Consider offering a small reward or privilege to the group with the highest score at the end of the game or even more importantly, played with the best attitudes and were the most cooperative.

Closure:

Conclude with a group reflection on the activity, discussing what strategies worked best and how the game helped reinforce the lesson content. Review the correct answers to any disputed questions and highlight effective teamwork and fair play observed during the game.

Assessment:

Evaluate students based on their engagement, ability to recall and locate the correct answers quickly, and their adherence to the rules of fair play.

Assess how effectively they worked as a team and managed the physical aspect of the game in relation to academic goals and expected behavior.

Sample Lesson Activity: $1,000 Dollar Pyramid

Objective:
"$1,000 Dollar Pyramid" is a vocabulary or content review game that challenges students to describe and guess words effectively under time constraints. Modeled after the classic game show, this activity fosters communication skills, quick thinking, and teamwork.

Materials:
- A visual representation of a pyramid divided into sections (e.g., using a smart board, whiteboard, or a large poster), with sections labeled with point values (100, 100, 200, 200, 500). Google $1,000 pyramid for examples to look at.
- A list of vocabulary words or key concepts prepared by the teacher, tailored to different difficulty levels according to point values and student age.
- Timer or stopwatch for tracking time limits.
- Optional but adds to the atmosphere-$1,000 game show music from YouTube.

Activity Overview:
Students work in pairs, with one student facing the pyramid (board) and the other with their back to it. The student facing the board provides verbal clues (without using the actual word) to help their partner guess the word or concept displayed. Each correct guess scores the points associated with that section of the pyramid, with higher points for more difficult words.

Setup Instructions:

1. Set up the pyramid on the board or a poster with the designated point values for each section.
2. Prepare a list of words or concepts and assign them to the appropriate sections based on difficulty. Changing words or phrases out each time students rotate. Be sure to go over possible clue choices after each round.
3. Organize students into pairs and position them so one is facing the board and the other cannot see it.

Rules of the Game:

1. The student facing the board sees the word and gives clues to their partner, trying to make them say the word without using it directly.
2. Each pair has 1 minute to guess as many words as possible in the first round, with subsequent rounds decreasing in time. Go over clue options after each round to assess what students used for their peer group.
3. After each half-round, students switch roles, so each gets a chance to give clues and guess.
4. Update the pyramid with new words for each rotation to maintain the challenge.
5. The teacher monitors the process, ensuring clues are appropriate and tallying points for each correct guess. Use the honor system here—too hard for the teacher to assess scores accurately. Not playing for a true winner but for fun to see how students did.

Activity Variations:

+ Introduce "steal" rounds where pairs can steal points from another pair if they guess a word that the original pair missed.

+ Use thematic categories for different rounds to cover various subjects or topics.
+ Include a "double or nothing" option where teams can risk their current round points to guess a particularly hard word or phrase.

Things to Consider:
+ Enhance vocabulary acquisition and application through active use of synonyms, definitions, and descriptions.
+ Develop critical listening and speaking skills as students must articulate and interpret clues quickly.

Scoring and Competition:
+ Assign points corresponding to the pyramid sections, more points for more difficult words.
+ Keep a running total of each team's points, with a bonus for the team that scores the most points in the fastest time.

Closure:
Review the game by discussing strategies that were effective, new vocabulary learned, and how the challenge of describing and guessing under pressure can be applied to other learning situations. Highlight outstanding performances and teamwork.

Assessment:
Evaluate students based on their ability to communicate clearly, use vocabulary effectively, and work cooperatively under pressure. Assess their engagement level and how well they adapted strategies to succeed in the game. Perhaps provide a written assessment as an exit ticket using the game questions or vocabulary.

Sample Lesson Activity: "Build It"

Objective:
"Build It," is a hands-on, creative activity designed to enhance students' understanding of a wide range of subjects by constructing physical models that represent concepts or themes from the curriculum. This project is suitable for any grade level and can be adapted to any subject area, from history and science to literature and mathematics.

Materials:
- Construction materials such as cardboard, construction paper, bulletin board paper, tape, modeling clay, fabric, and any recyclable items.
- Art supplies like markers, paint, glue, and scissors.
- Additional thematic materials depending on the subject that students can come up with to add something cool to what they create.

Activity Overview:
Students will use a variety of materials to build manipulatives or models that represent specific themes or concepts discussed in class. Whether it's a historical event, a scientific concept, a literary scene, or a mathematical principle, the physical creation of these concepts helps to solidify students' understanding and retention of academic content.

Setup Instructions:
1. Introduce the project and discuss the concept or theme that students will be building.
2. Divide students into groups based on the number of projects or aspects of the concept. Could be done whole class or each class or group gets a specified wall.
3. Provide a variety of building and craft materials.

4. Designate areas in the classroom for different groups to work on their projects.

Rules of the Activity:
1. Each group selects or is assigned a specific part of the broader topic to build. For example, one group builds the windmill or the rollercoaster etc.
2. Groups plan their models, considering how best to represent their assigned concepts physically. Using resources such as textbooks, visuals, online websites to help design their product. Nothing is off the table here – creativity and imagination to create something awesome is key.
3. Students begin constructing their models, using the provided materials to creatively interpret their topics.
4. Once completed, each group will present their model to the class, explaining how it represents the concept or theme and the choices they made during construction.

Activity Variations:
+ For classes meeting multiple times or across different periods, have students build upon previous groups' work, enhancing and expanding the models.
+ Introduce challenges where groups must incorporate specific elements or materials into their models.
+ Allow groups to combine their models into a large, class-wide project where all the pieces connect into a comprehensive display.

Things to Consider:
+ Encourage collaboration and problem-solving as students figure out how to best represent their concepts.

- Develop planning and project management skills as groups must design, organize, and execute their construction within a limited timeframe.
- While the primary focus is on participation and learning, you can introduce elements of competition by having class votes on the most creative, most accurate, or most detailed models.
- Include a written portion where students add a summary write up explaining what was built and some facts or history behind it, adding a literacy component.

Closure:

Conclude the activity with a classroom exhibition where each group presents their model or the whole class discusses their favorite aspects of what was created. Showcasing and spotlighting the creativity and originality of what was built. Discuss what was learned through the process and how these physical representations help enhance understanding of the topic. Reflect on the teamwork and creativity displayed during the project.

Assessment:

Evaluate students based on their engagement with the project, their ability to work collaboratively, and the creativity and accuracy of their final models. Assess how well they understood and interpreted the assignment, and how effectively they communicated their concepts through their constructions.

Sample Lesson Activity: Create Your Own Company

Objective:

"Create Your Own Company" is an expansive project where students assume the role of CEOs to conceive and develop a mock business or nonprofit organization. This multidisciplinary activity incorporates elements of economics, mathematics, writing, financial planning, advertising, and more, providing students with a practical application of these concepts as they create a realistic business plan that could potentially be implemented. This activity can be scaled down to fit the needs of younger learners simplifying or differentiating various aspects to make the project more manageable.

Materials:
+ Computers with internet access for research and presentation.
+ Software for document creation and graphic design (e.g., Google Slides, PowerPoint, Canva, AI Generators).
+ Art supplies for creating mock-ups of marketing materials.
+ Writing materials for drafting business plans and correspondence.

Activity Overview:
Students will develop a mock company or nonprofit organization from the ground up, starting with an idea that benefits the community. They will engage in every aspect of business creation, from planning and financial strategizing to marketing and public relations, culminating in a detailed business proposal that includes digital and physical promotional materials.

Setup Instructions:
1. Introduce the concept of creating a company, discussing the various components of a business plan.
2. Allow students to brainstorm different business ideas, focusing on community service or addressing specific needs. Ideas could include toys and blankets for sick children in the local hospital, school supplies for the local elementary schools, mowing lawn for the elderly, going to read to folks at the nursing homes or

providing them with blankets and slippers, or items for Mom's with newborn babies at the hospital for example.

3. Explain the range of materials they might produce, including emails to raise financial resources, flyers, advertisements, company logo with a slogan, and a mock website created on Power-Point, Google Docs/Slides, or Canva.

Rules of the Activity:

1. Each student or group selects a unique business idea and outlines their goals and target audience.
2. Students research their chosen industry and potential community impact, gathering data to support their business plan.
3. Participants draft a detailed business plan that includes financial strategies, marketing plans, and operational procedures.
4. Students create mock promotional materials, such as logos, flyers, and a mock website.
5. Throughout the project, students must draft, revise, and finalize professional emails discussing their business with hypothetical stakeholders being sure to analyze real-life examples of business documents to make theirs look authentic.

Activity Variations:

+ Introduce real-world constraints such as budget limits or specific community needs to increase the challenge.
+ Allow students to present their business plans to local entrepreneurs or administrative leaders in your school for feedback.

Things to Consider:

+ In a "Shark Tank" style, invite teachers or administration to listen to presentations and pick the student businesses that they would invest in.

- Enhance research and technology skills through the creation of digital and print materials through the creation of mock flyers with logos, QR codes to raise financial resources, mock advertising on t-shirts or mugs using online apps.
- Improve literacy and communication skills through professional writing and presentations to the class or other adults in the building.

Scoring and Competition:
- Have students or external judges rate each business based on creativity, feasibility, and the thoroughness of the plan. Thinking as though they were investors looking to get involved.
- Provide awards for categories such as "Most Innovative," "Best Presentation," and "Community Impact."

Closure:
Conclude the project with student presentations, where they showcase their business plans and promotional materials. Discuss what was learned through the process and how these skills can be applied in real-world scenarios.

Assessment:
Evaluate students on the creativity and viability of their business ideas, the clarity and detail of their business plans, and the professionalism of their communications and marketing materials. Assess their ability to integrate knowledge from various disciplines to create a comprehensive business proposal.

Sample Lesson Activity: Create a Board Game

Objective:
"Create a Board Game" encourages students to apply their knowledge of a subject by designing a custom board game that incorporates key

themes and concepts from their studies. This creative project not only tests their understanding but also fosters teamwork, strategic thinking, and artistic skills as they develop a playable board game.

Materials:
- Cardboard, poster board, or butcher paper for the game board.
- Markers, pens, and other art supplies for decorating.
- Dice, game pieces, and timers.
- Index cards or small pieces of paper for question cards.
- Resources for researching board games and content material.

Activity Overview:
Students work in cooperative learning groups to research existing board games for inspiration and then create their own game based on the unit content being studied. The game should include elements like a playing board, rules, game pieces, and cards with questions that integrate academic content. The end goal is for students to demonstrate their understanding of the subject through the mechanics and design of their game.

Setup Instructions:
1. Introduce the project by discussing popular board games and the elements that make those games engaging.
2. Assign students to groups and explain that their task is to create a board game based on specific academic content.
3. Provide materials and resources for game creation and research.

Rules of the Activity:
1. Each group must design a complete board game, including the board, rules, game pieces, and question cards.
2. The game should involve moving pieces on the board based on dice rolls or other mechanisms the student groups come up with.

3. Question cards should be integrated into gameplay, requiring players to answer questions related to the unit content to advance, gain points, or perform physical tasks like jumping jacks or running in place etc.
4. All elements of the game (pieces, cards, text) should be thematic and reflect the content being studied.
5. Groups must first create an outline of their game concept and review it with the teacher, then get peer feedback before finalizing their design.

Activity Variations:

+ Encourage groups to incorporate different game mechanics found in classic games like Monopoly (e.g., purchasing properties) or Chutes and Ladders (e.g., moving forward or backward based on answers).
+ Include creative physical activities in the game, such as performing exercises or tasks when certain cards are drawn.

Things to Consider:

+ Challenge students to be creative in how they incorporate educational content into the game. Show examples of real games and discuss how students could use ideas for their board games.
+ Develop teamwork and project management skills as they collaborate on game design and execution.

Scoring and Competition:

+ Once games are created, dedicate a class period to playing the games. Allow students to play each other's games and provide feedback.
+ Consider having prizes or awards for categories like "Most Creative," "Best Use of Theme," or "Most Educational."

Closure:

Conclude the project with a class discussion about the experience. Have students reflect on what they learned both from creating the games and from playing games designed by their peers. Discuss the educational value of the games and how this activity helped deepen their understanding of the content.

Assessment:

Evaluate students based on their engagement in the game creation process, the creativity and educational value of their games, and their ability to work collaboratively. Assess their understanding of the academic content as demonstrated through the game's questions and mechanics.

Sample Lesson Activity: Student Created Commercial or Movie Trailer

Objective:

"Student Created Commercial or Movie Trailer" offers students a dynamic platform to demonstrate their understanding of classroom topics through the creation of a commercial or movie trailer. This project encourages students to combine creativity with academic content, using digital media to craft engaging presentations that showcase their grasp of the material.

Materials:
+ Computers or tablets with video editing software (iMovie or other school-approved apps).
+ Video recording devices (smartphones or digital cameras).
+ Props and costumes as needed for filming.
+ Storyboard and script writing materials.

Activity Overview:
Students work in groups to develop a commercial or movie trailer about a specific unit of study, a character from a book, a historical event or a mathematical concept. The project involves scripting, filming, and editing a short video that incorporates educational content in an entertaining format. The activity is designed to enhance students' digital literacy and presentation skills while allowing them to creatively express their knowledge. This is perfect for a unit project assessment.

Setup Instructions:
1. Introduce the project and discuss examples of commercials and movie trailers to give students a clear idea of the format.
2. Assign students to groups and provide them with a specific topic related to the current unit of study.
3. Distribute storyboard and script writing materials to help groups plan their videos.

Rules of the Activity:
1. Each group selects or is assigned a specific topic to explore through their video.
2. Students research their topic and create an outline and script that incorporates key information into the commercial or trailer format.
3. Groups plan and film their video, using props, costumes, and settings as needed to enhance their presentation.
4. After initial filming, groups share their videos for peer review, receiving feedback on how to improve their work.
5. Students make any necessary edits to their videos based on the feedback and prepare for a final presentation.

Activity Variations:

- Include specific challenges, such as using certain vocabulary words, including a twist in the plot, or presenting a mathematical concept in a real-world scenario.
- Allow students to use different genres or film styles to match their creative vision (e.g., horror, comedy, documentary).

Things to Consider:

- Encourage creativity and critical thinking as students translate academic content into a compelling narrative.
- Develop technical skills in video production, including filming techniques, sound editing, and visual effects.
- Enhance teamwork and project management skills as groups collaborate on a complex creative project.

Scoring and Competition:

- Host a viewing party where videos are showcased to the class or a wider audience provide popcorn to make the experience feel like going to the movies!
- Consider having awards for categories like "Best Use of Educational Content," "Most Creative," "Best Editing," and "Audience Favorite."

Closure:

Conclude the project with a class discussion about the creative process and the various ways students chose to interpret their topics. Reflect on the skills learned through the project and how these skills can be applied in other educational or real-world contexts.

Assessment:

Evaluate students based on their ability to effectively communicate their assigned topics through video, the creativity of their approach, the quality of their final product, and their ability to incorporate academic content meaningfully. Assess their teamwork and the development of their technical skills in digital media production.

Sample Lesson Activity: STICKY NOTES!

Objective:
"STICKY NOTES!" is fun an interactive lesson activity designed to engage students in deep thinking and discussion around content-based questions. By using sticky notes for responses, students can visually explore multiple perspectives and evidence-based answers, fostering a richer understanding of the material. Perfect for all subject areas and easily scaled to meet the needs of any age level.

Materials:
+ Sticky notes in various colors.
+ Markers or pens.
+ Posters or designated wall space where questions will be posted.

Activity Overview:
Students will respond to content-related questions by writing their answers on sticky notes and placing them around the posted questions. This activity encourages individual thinking and peer collaboration, as students then group and discuss the answers, debating merits based on evidence provided. It's particularly effective for exploring questions with multiple correct answers and to look at a variety of viewpoints.

Setup Instructions:
1. Prior to class, select and post essential content questions around the classroom related to the current unit of study.
2. Provide stacks of sticky notes and writing materials at each question station.

3. Organize students into individual or small groups, depending on class size and the nature of the activity.

Rules of the Activity:
1. Each student or group starts at a question station with a stack of sticky notes.
2. Students write their answers on the sticky notes and stick them around the posted question.
3. After a set time, students move to the next station or rotate in an orderly manner.
4. Once all questions have responses, groups review all sticky note answers and choose the one they believe is best, discussing why it stands out based on evidence or reasoning.
5. Facilitate a class discussion where groups share their chosen answers and the rationale behind their choices.
6. Enhance critical thinking and evidence-based reasoning as students must defend their choices.

Activity Variations:
+ Use different colored sticky notes for different types of responses (e.g., blue for facts, pink for opinions).
+ Allow students to add rebuttals or additional evidence to others' sticky notes to further debate and discuss answers.

Things to Consider:
+ Develop communication skills through discussion and debate.
+ Promote organizational skills as students categorize and prioritize information.

Scoring and Competition:
+ Optionally, award points for the most compelling answer at each station, based on class votes or teacher discretion.

+ Recognize groups for insightful contributions or particularly well-supported answers.

Closure:

Wrap up the activity by reflecting on the diversity of answers and the importance of supporting opinions with evidence. Discuss how this exercise helped enhance their understanding of the topic and improved their analytical skills.

Assessment:

Evaluate students based on their ability to articulate answers clearly, use evidence effectively, and engage constructively in discussions. Assess how well they understood the content and could apply it to answer questions creatively and thoughtfully.

Sample Lesson Activity: Speed Dating

Objective:

"Speed Dating" is an activity designed to enhance students' understanding and retention of key concepts from readings or unit studies. By discussing their insights in a fast-paced cooperative peer-grouping format, students solidify their knowledge and pick up new information from their peers, fostering a deeper understanding of the subject matter.

Materials:

+ Chairs or desks arranged in rows facing each other.
+ Timer or buzzer for managing discussion time.
+ Notepads and pens for students to jot down important points.

Activity Overview:

Students first review or study a text or topic individually, then gather in a "speed dating" setup where they exchange information with multiple

189

partners in quick succession. This format not only helps students articulate their understanding clearly and concisely but also exposes them to diverse perspectives and insights from their classmates. Allotting time after each round to jot down new information learned and to use with the next partner.

Setup Instructions:
1. Have students individually read a text or review materials from a unit of study.
2. Ask them to compile a list of key points or insights they find important. Could modify for a mathematical concept by having students complete math problems in a given time to share with each other.
3. Arrange the classroom with chairs or desks in rows facing each other to facilitate quick exchanges between students.

Rules of the Activity:
1. Pair students and set the timer for a brief discussion round (e.g., 15 seconds per student).
2. One student in each pair discusses their points until the timer ends, then the other student shares their insights in the next round.
3. After both have spoken, allow 30 seconds for both students to add any new information to their lists that they learned from their partner.
4. Students then rotate to a new partner and the cycle repeats for several rounds.
5. After multiple rounds, bring the whole group together for a collective sharing session where students can pop in and share one point from their list.
6. Implement a rule where students must wait for five others to share before they can contribute again to ensure wide participation.

7. Conclude with a "writing dump" where students write down everything they can recall from the discussions.

Activity Variations:
+ Introduce themed rounds where students focus on specific aspects of the content, such as themes, characters, or historical impacts.
+ Use a "challenge" round where students can ask their partner a question that they think is difficult to answer.

Things to Consider:
+ Enhance students' oral communication skills and ability to think on their feet. Be sure to model to the whole group how the activity will work.
+ Encourage detailed note-taking and active listening as students must quickly discern and jot down new information.

Scoring and Competition:
+ Optionally, keep track of how many new pieces of information students gather from their peers, rewarding those who collect the most.

Closure:
Conclude with a "writing dump" where students write down everything they can recall from the discussions. This helps reinforce their memory of the content and provides a measure of what they learned through the activity.

Assessment:
Evaluate students based on the accuracy of information in their final written summaries. Assess their engagement in discussions and their ability to articulate and expand upon their knowledge. This

comprehensive approach provides insight into both their oral and written command of the topic.

Sample Lesson Activity: Drops in a Bucket

Objective:

"Drops in a Bucket" is an energetic, movement-based activity designed to transform traditional worksheet tasks into an interactive and collaborative classroom competition. By incorporating physical activity with academic challenges, this lesson enhances engagement and teamwork as students race to answer questions using their classroom resources.

Materials:

- Containers or buckets labeled with group numbers.
- Strips of paper or cut-out paper "water drops" for writing answers.
- Markers or pens for writing.
- Smartboard or large display for posting questions.
- Resources such as textbooks, notebooks, and folders.

Activity Overview:

Students are divided into groups, each with a corresponding answer bucket on the opposite side of the room. Questions (Ex. 1-10) are displayed all at the same time via smartboard, and groups must work together to write answers on paper strips or "drops" that they get from the teacher. A designated "runner" from each group then races to deliver these answers to the teacher for verification. Correct answers are dropped in the group's bucket, while incorrect ones are returned for revision. Once an answer is dropped in the group's bucket the runner gets another drop paper from the teacher for the next question.

Setup Instructions:

1. Arrange seating by grouping students and placing corresponding answer containers across the room.
2. Prepare paper strips or have students cut out paper "water drops" for students to write their answers.
3. Display questions on the smartboard, ensuring visibility for all groups.

Rules of the Activity:

1. The teacher starts the activity by displaying the first question.
2. Each group discusses and writes their answer on a paper drop.
3. A runner from each group quickly takes the completed drop to the teacher for checking.
4. If the answer is correct, the runner drops it in their bucket and retrieves a new drop for the next question. If incorrect, the runner returns to the group for further discussion.
5. The game continues until all questions are answered or the time limit expires. Groups gain points for correct answers within the time limit.

Activity Variations:

+ Introduce bonus questions that are worth more points or challenges that require multiple steps to solve.
+ Allow teams to use "lifelines," such as asking for a hint or skipping a question.
+ Include physical challenges, like doing a quick exercise before picking up a new drop.

Things to Consider:

+ Encourage critical thinking and rapid problem-solving as groups must quickly decide and write down their answers.
+ Develop teamwork and communication, as groups need to work efficiently to discuss and relay information.

Scoring and Competition:

+ Track how many correct drops each group collects within the given time.
+ Award additional points for the first group to answer all questions correctly or for the most creative solutions to complex questions.

Closure:

Conclude with a group discussion about the activity, focusing on what strategies led to success and what challenges were encountered. Review the correct answers to each question, emphasizing the learning objectives covered in the activity.

Assessment:

Evaluate students based on their participation, accuracy of answers, and ability to collaborate effectively under pressure. Assess their engagement and understanding of the content through both their written responses and their discussion contributions during the activity.

Sample Lesson Activity: Children's Book

Objective:

"Children's Book" is an imaginative and engaging activity where students apply their literacy skills and creativity to showcase key content from a unit of study into a children's story. This task encourages students to transform complex topics into engaging, understandable narratives, which helps deepen their comprehension and retention of the material.

Materials:

+ Paper and writing utensils for drafting stories.
+ Computers with access to AI image generators and design software like using Canva for creating illustrations.

- Examples of popular children's books for reference.
- Guidelines for story structure and outline development.

Activity Overview:
Students either individually or in small groups develop a short children's story based on a specific educational theme or content area. The project involves creating a narrative that simplifies and personifies concepts—such as fractions in a pizza parlor scenario or historical events through a character's eyes—making them relatable and understandable for younger audiences.

Setup Instructions:
1. Introduce the project by discussing various successful children's books, highlighting key elements that make them effective.
2. Assign themes or units of study for the students to base their stories on.
3. Provide resources and tools for writing and illustrating the stories, including access to digital platforms for those opting to use technology.

Rules of the Activity:
1. Students begin by brainstorming and outlining their stories, focusing on how best to convey the chosen content in a simple narrative that young kids could better understand.
2. Each group or individual must create a story outline and pitch it to the "publisher"—the teacher—for initial feedback.
3. Incorporate peer review sessions where students present their outlines to another group and receive suggestions.
4. Develop a rough draft of the story or content, including both text and illustrations, ensuring that the content aligns closely with the educational objectives.

5. Finalize the story and prepare for a class presentation, where each group or individual conducts an "author reading" mimicking professional book readings.

Activity Variations:

+ Encourage students to use various methods for their illustrations, including hand-drawn art, digital images, or mixed media and AI image generators.
+ Allow advanced students to create interactive or animated versions of their stories using digital tools.

Things to Consider:

+ Enhance artistic abilities through the creation of illustrations that complement and enhance the text.
+ Students work on presentation skills through the final reading and discussion session.

Scoring and Competition:

+ While the primary focus is on learning and creativity, consider recognizing stories for creativity, accuracy, and clarity in presenting the content.
+ Optionally, have a class vote for categories like "Most Creative," "Best Illustration," or "Best Understanding of Content."

Closure:

Wrap up the project with a class discussion on the different approaches to the story or content creation and the impact of visual and narrative elements on teaching complex ideas. Review and critique final products, providing constructive feedback and celebrating students' efforts.

Assessment:

Evaluate students based on their ability to research, outline, and communicate the academic content creatively and clearly in their stories.

Assess their storytelling techniques, clarity, effectiveness of illustrations, and overall presentation during the reading session.

Sample Lesson Activity: Mock/Fake Content Social Media

Objective:
"Mock/Fake Content Social Media" creatively integrates students' interest in social media with academic learning objectives. This activity encourages students to create educational mock social media accounts that convey content knowledge through posts, photos, and videos, using platforms and styles they are familiar with, such as Instagram or TikTok. The goal is to create the account as if the account is teaching about a content theme using descriptions and images in a social media format. This activity can be done by hand or by using school approved multi-media and technology apps.

Materials:
+ Construction paper, markers, and colored pencils (if done by hand).
+ Computers or tablets with internet access.
+ Access to applications like Google Slides, PowerPoint, or Canva.
+ Guidelines for social media post creation, including advice on visuals, text, and hashtags.

Activity Overview:
Foster digital literacy and design skills as students use tech tools to create authentic-looking social media posts. Students design a mock/fake social media page dedicated to a specific educational topic, such as science facts, historical events, or mathematical concepts. This project combines literacy, creativity, technology, and real-world application skills as students develop posts that are both informative and engaging.

Setup Instructions:
1. Introduce the concept of the activity and discuss popular social media formats and their typical content and layout.
2. If you use technology, Canva (which is free) has social media templates already set up for the students to use. This is a great resource.
3. Explain the educational goal of creating a mock social media page that teaches followers about a specific subject.
4. Assign or let students choose their specific topics or subjects for their social media page.

Rules of the Activity:
1. Students plan and create a series of posts for their assigned topic using the designated digital tools.
2. Each post should include a visual element (photo, infographic, or video), a descriptive text explaining the content, and relevant hashtags to enhance learning and engagement. These can be self-generated or through the use of the AI generator tool on Canva or found online and implemented onto their posts.
3. Encourage students to ensure that their content is accurate, informative, and presented in a way that mimics real social media accounts.
4. Students must also consider their audience, aiming to make their posts accessible and educational for peers.

Activity Variations:
- Allow students to choose different social media platforms to focus on, adapting their content to fit the style of each platform.
- Include a component where students can interact with each other's pages by posting a printed copy around the room as if students were "scrolling social media" and leaving comments or questions that the page owner must respond to.

- Challenge students to include interactive elements like quizzes or polls in their posts.
- Consider the audience—perhaps the account is geared towards teaching younger students about the given theme or topic. This would mean students would need to simplify the content which is a great way to retain it themselves.

Things to Consider:
- Develop research and critical thinking skills as they gather and synthesize information to be shared.
- Enhance creativity through the visual and textual interpretation of educational content.
- Conduct a class review of the social media pages, with students presenting their work. Again, this could be printed versions posted around the room and students view them as if they are "scrolling" social media.
- Offer awards in categories such as "Best Design," "Most Informative," and "Most Creative Hashtags."

Closure:
Wrap up the activity by reflecting on what students learned through the process of creating and viewing each other's social media pages. Discuss the impact of social media on learning and information dissemination. Review the most successful aspects of the pages created and how these techniques can be applied to real-world digital communication.

Assessment:
Evaluate students based on the clarity and accuracy of their content, the creativity and relevance of their visuals and descriptions, and their overall engagement with the project. Assess their ability to communicate effectively through a modern medium and their understanding of the subject matter as demonstrated in their posts.

Sample Lesson Activity: Group Tic Tac Toe

Objective:
"Group Tic Tac Toe" turns the classic game into an educational tool, adaptable for any subject area and suitable for students of all ages. This activity incorporates quick-thinking challenges with the strategic game play of Tic Tac Toe, encouraging students to compete in teams to answer questions and earn their marks on the game board.

Materials:
- Whiteboard or poster board set up with multiple Tic Tac Toe grids.
- Markers for writing on the board.
- A set of questions related to the subject matter being reviewed.
- Scorecard to track team points.

Activity Overview:
Students are divided into small groups and assigned to be either Team X or Team O. Questions are posed by the teacher, and groups compete to answer correctly first. This could be done by grabbing a physical object like an expo marker once the group has an answer or simply having the whole group hold their hands up like on a roller coaster while also showing the answer. Turning the whole activity into a group experience. The winning team chooses where to place their mark on a Tic Tac Toe grid, aiming to get three in a row. The activity continues with groups rotating opponents and playing against other groups, enhancing engagement through competition and strategic thinking.

Setup Instructions:
1. Prepare the classroom by drawing several Tic Tac Toe grids on the whiteboard or on poster boards around the room.
2. Divide students into small groups and assign each group as either X or O.

3. Write questions related to the unit of study and decide on the sequence of asking them.

Rules of the Activity:

1. The teacher poses a question to all teams either verbally or by posting it where all can see.
2. Teams discuss and the first to answer correctly gets the opportunity to place their mark on one of the Tic Tac Toe grids.
3. Teams aim to get three of their marks in a row (horizontal, vertical, or diagonal) to win that grid.
4. After each round, teams rotate to face a new opponent and continue the game.
5. Points are awarded for each grid won, and the teacher updates the scorecard after each round.

Activity Variations:

+ Include "power-up" questions that allow a team to place two marks or remove an opponent's mark. This adds energy to the game!
+ Implement themed questions that align with different subjects or current events aligning with student interests to keep the content fresh and relevant.

Things to Consider:

+ Encourage teamwork and cooperative strategy formulation within groups.
+ Enhance critical thinking and spatial awareness as teams strategize their moves on the grid.

Scoring and Competition:

+ Keep a visible scorecard to track which teams win each grid.
+ Award additional points for teams that win multiple games in a row or conquer the most challenging questions.

Closure:

End the activity with a discussion on strategies that were effective and what teams learned about working together. Review key topics from the questions asked during the game and highlight any recurring themes or important takeaways.

Assessment:

Evaluate students based on their ability to actively participate, use knowledge effectively to answer questions, and work strategically within their teams. Consider their engagement level, the accuracy of their responses, and their ability to collaborate towards a common goal.

Sample Lesson Activity: Zombie Apocalypse (StoryLine Simulations)

Objective:

"Zombie Apocalypse (StoryLine Simulations)" immerses students in a thrilling narrative where they apply their knowledge to survive in a fictional scenario. This activity combines elements of role-playing with academic review, utilizing technology and creative storytelling to enhance student engagement and comprehension.

Materials:

- Computers with Internet access for script and image generation (AI tools like ChatGPT, Canva).
- PowerPoint, Google Slides, or other presentation software.
- Sound effects and background music (access to YouTube or similar).
- Decorations to enhance the thematic experience (dim lighting, butcher paper, thematic signs).
- Markers or tape to number desks.

Activity Overview:

Students work in cooperative groups within a dynamic, story-driven simulation that pits them against challenges such as escaping zombies or solving critical problems to progress in the game. This can be a teacher-controlled narrative or created to be self-paced through tech apps such as Near Pod or a similar tech tool. Points are awarded for correct answers, influencing the group's chances of survival in the storyline. The activity and storyline can be self-generated, or the teacher can use AI-generated scripts to create engaging and coherent narratives, with thematic visual and audio elements to deepen immersion. For example, asking AI to write a script for a teacher to use as a superhero, zombie, or aliens attack story line with content questions infused into the story.

Setup Instructions:

1. Set up the classroom environment to match the Zombie Apocalypse theme, using dim lighting and thematic decorations.
2. Prepare a storyline with different scenarios using an AI script generator like ChatGPT, linking each part of the story to review questions or tasks that students need to solve.
3. Create themed slides that set the stage for each scenario and include relevant questions.
4. Set up a sound system for background noises and music to enhance the atmosphere. Playing YouTube zombie noises with dim lighting is a great way to hook the students and take student engagement to the next level.

Rules of the Activity:

1. Introduce the storyline to students and explain the rules: correct answers help them escape dangers and gain points; incorrect answers result in penalties.
2. Students begin at their numbered desks. Each round of questions corresponds to different scenarios in the storyline.

3. After answering a question, students have 20 seconds to move to a new seat as directed, simulating movement within the story's environment.

4. Randomly call out seat numbers after each round for bonus challenges or penalties (e.g., gaining extra shield points, encountering zombies).

5. Use AI tools to assist with generating story content. and questions in real- time, keeping the narrative exciting and unpredictable.

Activity Variations:

+ Incorporate different story themes like treasure hunts, zombies, superhero rescues, or alien invasions to cater to varied interests.

+ Allow students to choose their path in the story based on majority decisions in their groups, leading to different challenges and outcomes.

+ Include physical activities or tasks as part of the challenges for a more interactive experience.

+ Depending on student age and academic level, allow students to use the content as a second day activity to make their own storylines with infused questions as an additional project. Students use AI tools to assist with generating story content and questions keeping the narrative exciting and unpredictable.

+ Have students build their slides with animations and sound effects along with turning in their script and question outline.

+ The teacher can then take some of the best ideas and use them later in the year for other content areas.

Things to Consider:

+ Enhance critical thinking and problem-solving skills as students apply knowledge to answer questions under pressure.

+ Develop teamwork and communication within groups as they strategize the best responses and movements.
+ Foster creativity and quick decision-making in response to evolving story developments.

Scoring and Competition:
+ Track points for correct answers, successful escapes, and strategic decisions that benefit the group.
+ Offer rewards or recognition for teams that demonstrate exceptional problem-solving or creative tactics.

Closure:
Conclude the simulation with a debriefing session, discussing the outcomes and the decisions made by students throughout the game. Reflect on the learning points and how the activity helped in understanding the reviewed content. Solicit feedback on the experience and any suggestions for future simulations.

Assessment:
Evaluate students based on their participation, accuracy of their answers, and their ability to work collaboratively with peers. Assess their engagement level and understanding of the subject matter as demonstrated through their responses and interaction with the storyline.

List of Current Lesson Ideas

Relationship/ Community Activities:

1. Head, Shoulders, Knees, COLOR!
2. Tower of Terror
3. The Almost Impossible Cup Pyramid

4. The Scribe
5. Face-off
6. Puzzle Maker

Instructional Content Strategies:

7. The Quiet Debate
8. 3D Wall Timeline
9. 3D Math Wall (modified #8)
10. Grading Papers
11. Create-a-Test!
12. Quick Hands
13. Headbands Vocabulary Review
14. Bluffing
15. The Great Literacy Race
16. 4-Corners Review
17. Is it TRUE? (Based on the Netflix gameshow "is it CAKE?!")
18. Boom, Clap, GRAB!
19. Pop It (Balloons Needed)
20. 100's Chart Race
21. FAST CASH
22. Be the Teacher Podcast
23. Student-Teacher Videocast
24. Unit/Topic Sketch-Note
25. Sketch-Noting Using AI Imaging
26. Gallery Walk
27. Movie Poster Advertisement
28. Creative Comic Strip
29. Grudge Ball
30. Human Bingo
31. The Bag Game

32. Go Fish / Old Maid
33. Splat Review
34. $1,000 Dollar Pyramid
35. "Build It"
36. Create Your Own Company
37. Create a Board Game
38. Student Created Commercial or Movie Trailer
39. STICKY NOTES!
40. Speed Dating
41. Drops in a Bucket
42. Children's Book
43. Mock/Fake Content Social Media
44. Group Tic Tac Toe
45. Zombie Apocalypse (StoryLine Simulations)

CHAPTER 8

~

The Teachers We Remember

"Every day is a new opportunity to make a difference."

A Vision Unseen: Walt Disney

In the Alsheimer household, we love all things Disney. The global renown of Disney and Disney World is no secret, but many people are unaware of how it all began. As a young child, Walt Disney had a wild imagination and a fascination with drawing. He would often sit outside, gaze up at the stars, and let his imagination take flight. His passion and vision resulted in something amazing.

His father, along with many others, however, did not share Walt Disney's passion and vision. In the beginning, Walt struggled to get his business off the ground, and many thought his ideas of creating a company of story characters was laughable. Even when Walt came up with the idea of Mickey Mouse, hundreds of people continued to turn down the idea of the mouse as he pursued his vision and dream.

As the story of Walt Disney's journey unfolds, we all know the ending. His vision and dream eventually became a reality. His business took off and led to a multi-billion-dollar company with theme parks spread around the world. His passion and purpose for magic have inspired little children and people all around the world to dream big and realize that something great is out there if they only have the presence to wish upon a star and never give up in their pursuit of that dream.

The more I learned about Walt Disney's journey, the more I could see a direct correlation to education and teaching. As teachers walk through the doors and hallways of their schools with the ultimate goal to inspire the next generation, that passion can feel like an unshared dream. Like Walt Disney experienced, the world may not fully see and appreciate the vision and purpose of educators. But if we continue to dream big and let our actions and passion guide us, that vision will lead to inspiring the hearts and minds of the next generation, leaving a lasting impact that long precedes us.

That is why this book was created—to share a new vision of collaborative instructional development that allows teachers to focus on and reignite that fire for teaching. By taking some of the pressure off the shoulders of teachers, we enable their passion and purpose to thrive. Like the magic of Disney inspiring people all around the world, educators inspire and will be remembered years after our careers end. Our names and the experiences we created will be spoken around dinner tables, on car rides, or at random moments in time as, "I remember when…" Those impactful moments are created in the classroom with engaging experiences, in the hallways during moments when we build relationships, and through how we motivate students to realize their truest potential.

Transformative Teaching: A Willingness to Try

Teaching is a powerful job with a lasting impact: every day, you get the chance to change lives. But it's also a tough job, with a laundry list of to-dos, including the most important task of all: connecting with kids, building relationships, and creating engaging lessons that really stick. That's why the framework and vision in this book was established. It's about rethinking student engagement and our instruction process, to take some of the pressures off you, the teacher.

I once heard a story about a teacher talking to his class of students. He poured water into a glass then quite simply asked, "How much does this glass of water weigh?" As the class of students began to call out various weights that perhaps seemed accurate, the teacher shook his head, declining all possible responses. He paused, then began to teach a very valuable lesson. He explained that the weight of the glass was relative to how long you hold it. If you hold the glass for one minute, it's practically weightless. If you hold it for five minutes, it begins to feel heavy, and the longer you hold that glass, the weight becomes unbearable to the point of having to desperately drop the glass out of exhaustion. The teacher went on to discuss the purpose: when we hold onto something, the weight that once seemed so light begins to overpower us.

Just like in teaching, the weight of lesson planning and instructional development at first seems weightless. Once we stack on data-meetings, parent-meetings, grading, school events, and all the demands put on the shoulders of teachers, we quickly become overwhelmed. The weight becomes too heavy. Because of this, one of the most important and critical aspects of teaching–instructional planning–does not get the time and attention it deserves. Insufficient time to create highly effective and engaging activities eventually becomes the most challenging part of our job and seemingly all-consuming.

We know that lesson planning can be the toughest part of our jobs, sometimes dampening the vibrant atmosphere we strive for in our classrooms and schools. But here's the good news: it doesn't have to be this way. This book is your roadmap to changing the game. It's a creative blueprint designed for us, the teachers, to join forces in lesson planning. Together, we can level the stress and make room for the joy of teaching.

Let's turn the tide on the frustration that comes with an isolated, do-it-alone approach. With these pages as our guide, we learn to share the load and innovate the way we craft our lessons. The collaborative approach advocated for in this book should inspire us to look forward to instructional planning, tapping into the collective genius that thrives in our hallways. It's time to lighten our load and lift our spirits through collaboration, leveraging real professional development from within our school community to create something special that benefits us all.

Innovative Teaching

Let's get practical. Innovative teaching isn't about flashy gadgets or trendy buzzwords that come and go like the breeze—it's about great ideas that endure, are easily adaptable, and can be implemented daily. These ideas transcend specific content or grade-levels specific lessons, serving to build a tangible resource of lesson ideas that support teachers. The best part is, many of these ideas already exist in your school. While this book offers numerous lesson ideas to enhance student engagement in your classroom, the real and straightforward innovation lies in the framework and concept of a collaborative resource.

The key to making instructional planning more practical lies in utilizing the ideas within your own building and tapping into the expertise of all the professional educators who walk your halls. The experiences of your colleagues and that genuine professional development from within your school can revolutionize the classroom experience for both teachers and students. It's about leveraging the wisdom of teachers with years of experiences alongside fresh perspectives of new educators just starting their career. Together, we all contribute to creating a learning environment that is enjoyable, engaging and fosters a love of learning in students.

Collaboration is key. By openly sharing successes and challenges, we alleviate the burden for everyone involved. Picture planning a lesson with a network of fellow teachers—exchanging ideas, sharing resources, and preemptively addressing potential problems. This collaborative approach transforms teaching. It's about relying on each other to craft lessons that aren't merely informative, but also captivating and unforgettable.

The Magic of Collaboration

Just as Walt Disney envisioned, it's not just about the thrill of the rides, but the joy and passion of the people that truly make it magical. It's the cast members and their dedication to creating special moments that drive excitement and engagement. That same spark can illuminate our classrooms. It's time to view education from a fresh perspective, where the strength of our connections isn't just rhetoric; it's our mission. We're not merely changing how we teach; we're revolutionizing every corridor of our schools, every classroom, and every interaction into a vibrant atmosphere that rivals the energy of Disney World's streets.

We're enhancing student engagement not only through content-focused lessons, but also emphasizing classroom culture, community, and relationships. Students leave eager for more, asking, "Can we do that again tomorrow?" This is where the magic begins, where the classroom transforms, making every day an invitation to discover that learning is not just educational—it's exhilarating.

As the year progresses, we defy conventional norms and unlock the full potential of education. Our classrooms evolve into more than mere learning spaces; they become stages for impact and platforms for inspiration. Classroom disruptions fade while student engagement and learning thrive. Together, educators devise strategies that captivate our students' hearts and minds through creative, unconventional methods.

With a renewed shared vision, we adjust our focus toward collaborative planning and staff meetings. We exchange activities that cultivate a passion for learning and nurture a community eager for knowledge and progress. These are not mere exercises; they are milestones toward a classroom culture in which each lesson fosters both intellectual growth and character development.

The impact is profound and far-reaching, as school leaders pave the way for transforming our classrooms and schools into vibrant learning communities. Administrative and leadership teams amplify the excellence of our teachers by actively participating in professional growth initiatives. This new collaborative approach to instructional development offers the practical support and assistance teachers need to create enriching learning experiences for their students.

This revolution isn't just lifting the spirits of those in our classrooms; it is sending a shockwave of change throughout our entire school. Our halls now hum with a new, palpable energy that continues to gather momentum. Schools are no longer mere structures filled with routine learning; they have become the heart of our community, fostering curiosity, creativity, and collaborative learning. Teachers radiate genuine smiles reflecting the joy of teaching. No more sarcastic quips about "another day in paradise." Instead, we're actively shaping it, day by day. This isn't just a slogan; it's a lived experience where our passion propels us and our love for teaching sustains us.

How Do You Want to Be Remembered?

Back in the '90s, us '90s kids were truly dedicated to our favorite shows, embracing the adventure of live TV, complete with endless commercials—no streaming, no rewinds, just pure anticipation. Friday nights were sacred, hosting the iconic "TGIF" lineup, a cheerful echo of "Thank God It's Friday!" when shows like my favorite *Boy Meets World* reigned supreme. This show, a heartfelt journey through the eyes of a young boy and his family, shared stories of the everyday hurdles many kids encounter growing up. Among the cast was the unforgettable Mr. Feeny, a teacher whose wisdom reached far beyond textbooks.

Season after season, he was the guiding light in the storm of teenage adolescence.

The power of Mr. Feeny's character didn't just resonate then; it echoes even louder now. In the final episode, the four main student characters met Mr. Feeny in the classroom one last time. It became a place of heartfelt farewells, each student, one-by-one imparting a piece of their soul: "You were more of a father than my own Dad." "I'm not sure of my future, but I know I'm going to be a good person," and "You never gave up on me. Not even once. You're the best person I know."

Reflecting on those final moments, it's clear that Mr. Feeny's true lesson was never about grades. It was about the mark he left on their lives, the connections he forged, and the unwavering belief that every student mattered. He wasn't just teaching; he was nurturing a love for learning and a desire to be a better person. It wasn't test scores that were remembered, but the life-changing impact of a teacher who truly cared. This is the lasting gift of educators like Mr. Feeny, who inspire not just to educate, but to leave a profound mark on the hearts and minds of students.

Think about the kind of teacher you want to be. How do you want to be remembered? Like Mr. Feeny, the goal is to impact not just our student's lives in the moment, but to leave a lasting impression, formed through building relationships and academic growth. Those are the teachers we remember—the kind who not only educate, but inspire. By creating an environment in which connections are built and learning is engaging, we draw students in. We may have these students for only one year, but let's work together to make it a year that ignites a lifelong love of learning.

When we support each other, we don't just teach better, we grow together as professionals. Teaching is not only hard work, it's heart work, and people should always be at the center of our efforts. That's the essence of a strong school community and that's what this book is all about—simple, sustainable ways to become an outstanding teacher, not just individually, but as part of a cohesive team.

Just as Walt Disney had a vision of what "could be," we, too, share a new vision for instructional development, education, and the teaching and learning experience. However, our focus is not on what "could be," but on what "will be."

> Teaching is not only hard work, it's heart work, and people should always be at the center of our efforts.

Every day presents an opportunity to make a difference. Let's choose to rise together, create something special, and leave our mark. Let's be the teachers, educators, and leaders to remember!

About the Author

Jonathan Alsheimer is the unorthodox, energetic, and entertaining teacher who refuses to live a life of limitations and works with UFC Fighters, Celebrities, and Clothing Brands. In addition to being a passionate educator, Jonathan is an international keynote speaker and the best-selling author of "*NEXT LEVEL TEACHING.*"

Jonathan, taught at the world-renowned Fred Lynn Middle School, which was featured in two documentaries *Relentless* and *Relentless: Chasing Accreditation*, as the teacher who forged a partnership with UFC Fighter and light-weight contender Paul Felder to bring a message of never giving up, fighting for their education, and empowering the students to believe in themselves, all principles that Jonathan promotes in his classroom.

Jonathan Alsheimer also partnered with Fear the Fighter, an MMA clothing brand to establish a stop-bullying campaign. Jonathan Alsheimer didn't stop there and established a relationship with Drama, MTV reality star and CEO of *Young and Reckless* to promote and build student leaders in his school.

Jonathan, an educator in northern Virginia, has been featured on USA Channel 9 and NBC News for establishing a national give-back movement called "A Rae of Hope," started in his classroom to help pediatric patients in hospitals, which has now grown and been implemented in schools and classrooms across the nation.

As Jonathan always says, "Game-changing is not a cliche motto; it is a way of life...some talk about it while others live by it! **Connect with Jonathan at:** www.jonathanalsheimer.com or on social media at: @mr_alsheimer

More from ConnectEDD Publishing

Since 2015, ConnectEDD has worked to transform education by empowering educators to become better-equipped to teach, learn, and lead. What started as a small company designed to provide professional learning events for educators has grown to include a variety of services to help educators and administrators address essential challenges. ConnectEDD offers instructional and leadership coaching, professional development workshops focusing on a variety of educational topics, a roster of nationally recognized educator associates who possess hands-on knowledge and experience, educational conferences custom-designed to meet the specific needs of schools, districts, and state/national organizations, and ongoing, personalized support, both virtually and onsite. In 2020, ConnectEDD expanded to include publishing services designed to provide busy educators with books and resources consisting of practical information on a wide variety of teaching, learning, and leadership topics. Please visit us online at connecteddpublishing.com or contact us at: info@connecteddpublishing.com

Recent Publications:

Live Your Excellence: Action Guide by Jimmy Casas

Culturize: Action Guide by Jimmy Casas

Daily Inspiration for Educators: Positive Thoughts for Every Day of the Year by Jimmy Casas

Eyes on Culture: Multiply Excellence in Your School by Emily Paschall

Pause. Breathe. Flourish. Living Your Best Life as an Educator by William D. Parker

L.E.A.R.N.E.R. Finding the True, Good, and Beautiful in Education by Marita Diffenbaugh

Educator Reflection Tips Volume II: Refining Our Practice by Jami Fowler-White

Handle With Care: Managing Difficult Situations in Schools with Dignity and Respect by Jimmy Casas and Joy Kelly

Disruptive Thinking: Preparing Learners for Their Future by Eric Sheninger

Permission to be Great: Increasing Engagement in Your School by Dan Butler

Daily Inspiration for Educators: Positive Thoughts for Every Day of the Year, Volume II by Jimmy Casas

The 6 Literacy Levers: Creating a Community of Readers by Brad Gustafson

The Educator's ATLAS: Your Roadmap to Engagement by Weston Kieschnick

In This Season: Words for the Heart by Todd Nesloney, LaNesha Tabb, Tanner Olson, and Alice Lee

Leading with a Humble Heart: A 40-Day Devotional for Leaders by Zac Bauermaster

Recalibrate the Culture: Our Why...Our Work...Our Values by Jimmy Casas

Creating Curious Classrooms: The Beauty of Questions by Emma Chiappetta

Crafting the Culture: 45 Reflections on What Matters Most by Joe Sanfelippo and Jeffrey Zoul

Improving School Mental Health: The Thriving School Community Solution by Charle Peck and Dr. Cameron Caswell

Building Authenticity: A Blueprint for the Leader Inside You by Todd Nesloney and Tyler Cook

Connecting Through Conversation: A Playbook for Talking with Kids by Erika Bare and Tiffany Burns

The Dream Factory: Designing a Purposeful Life by Mark Trumbo

Stories Behind Stances: Creating Empathy Through Hearing "The Other Side" by Chris Singleton

Happy Eyes: All Things to All People by Ryan Tillman

The Generative Age Artificial Intelligence and the Future of Education by Alana Winnick

Recalibrate the Culture: Action Guide by Jimmy Casas

Leading with PEOPLE: A Six Pillar Framework for Fruitful Leadership by Zac Bauermaster

A School Leader's Guide to Reclaiming Purpose by Frederick C. Buskey

Foundations of an Elite Culture: Building Success with High Standards and a Positive Environment by David Arencibia

Personalize: Meeting the Needs of All Learners by Eric Sheninger and Nicki Slaugh

The Five Principles of Educator Professionalism: Rebuilding Trust in Schools by Nason Lollar

CønnectEDD
PUBLISHING